BREAD IN THE WILDERNESS

"And His disciples answered Him: from whence can anyone fill them here with bread in the wilderness?"

MARK, 8:4

A NEW DIRECTIONS BOOK

Thomas Merton

BREAD IN THE WILDERNESS

...NIS

...urice Malloy, O. C. S. O.
...l Bourne, O. C. S. O.
Imprimi Potest
Frater M. Gabriel Sortais, O. C. S. O.
Abbas Generalis

NIHIL OBSTAT

John M. A. Fearns, S. T. D.
Censor Librorum

IMPRIMATUR

✠ Francis Cardinal Spellman
Archbishop of New York

Copyright 1953 by Our Lady of Gethsemani Monastery

Acknowledgment: The photographs of "Le Devot Christ" at Perpignan, France, are by J. Comet and are reproduced in this volume and on the cover by his kind permission.

Manufactured in the United States of America.
New Directions Books are printed on acid-free paper.
Published simultaneously in Canada by Penguin Books Canada Limited.
First published clothbound by New Directions in 1953. First published as New Directions Paperbook 91 in 1960 and as a New Directions Classic in 1997.

Library of Congress Cataloging-in-Publication Data
Merton, Thomas, 1915-1968.
    Bread in the wilderness / Thomas Merton.
        p.   cm. — (A New Directions classic)
    Originally published: 1953.
    ISBN 0-8112-1348-X (alk. paper)
    1. Bible. O.T. Psalms—Criticism, interpretation, etc.   2. Spritual
    life—Catholic Church.   3. Catholic Church—Doctrines.
    I. Title.   II. Series: New Directions Classics.
    BS1430.2.M445   1997
    248.3—dc21   97-509
                                        CIP

New Direction Books are published for James Laughlin
by New Directions Publishing Corporation
80 Eighth Avenue, New York 10011

SECOND PRINTING

To Jean Danielou, S.J.

CONTENTS

The pictures in this book are of a famous Crucifix, venerated for centuries in a chapel adjoining the Cathedral of Perpignan, in Southern France. Nobody knows who carved this terrible masterpiece. No one is quite sure where it came from. Was it brought to Perpignan from Germany or Spain? Or was it, as most people believe, the work of an anonymous Catalan, living in Perpignan or in the nearby Pyrenees? Whatever may be the origin of the Devot Christ, there has probably never been a work of Christian art that so powerfully expressed the suffering of Christ on the Cross. This is indeed the Christ Whom the prophet Isaias described as a twisted root laid bare to the sun on the parched rocks of the desert. This is truly the Christ of whom Isaias cried: " There is no beauty in Him nor comeliness: and we have seen Him and there was no sightliness that we should be desirous of Him, despised and the most abject of men, a man of sorrows and acquainted with infirmity: . . . Surely He hath borne our infirmities and carried our sorrows, and we have thought Him as it were a leper, and one struck by God and afflicted." This too is the Christ of the twenty-first Psalm and of the other Psalms we discuss in this book. It is the Christ of the Dark Night of St John of the Cross. It is the Christ Who shares His agony with the mystics. And finally it is the Christ of our own time—the Christ of the bombed city and of the concentration camp. We have seen Him and we know Him well. This Devot Christ is the image of what the men of our time are doing to one another: for they are murdering Him in one another. But because there are many in whom He dies again, there are also many in whom He lives again, for Christ dies only in order to rise again from the dead. This picture, therefore is the picture of our Redeemer, the Saviour of the World. Of Him Isaias said, in the same fifty-third chapter of his prophecy: " He was wounded for our iniquities, He was bruised for our sins; the chastisement of our peace was upon Him, and by His bruises we are healed. All we like sheep have gone astray, every one hath turned aside into his own way: and the Lord hath laid upon Him the iniquity of us all."

Small wonder that this Devot Christ is sought out day by day by penitents and pilgrims in the French Catalan country. This Crucifix is held to be miraculous, to grant many favors to those possessed of pure devotion —ab los que tenan pura devocio. And there is a legend about Him. The bowed head is said to fall, each year, a fraction of an inch toward the chest. The Catalans say that when the chin finally comes to rest upon the chest, it will be the end of our world.

What is this book about? For whom is it written?

It is a book about the Psalms. The Psalms are perhaps the most significant and influential collection of religious poems ever written. They sum up the whole theology of the Old Testament. They have been used for centuries as the foundation for Jewish and Christian liturgical prayer. They still play a more important part than any other body of religious texts, in the public prayer of the Church. Benedictine and Cistercian monks chant their way through the entire Psalter, once a week. Those whose vocation in the Church is prayer find that they live on the Psalms—for the Psalms enter into every department of their life. Monks get up to chant Psalms in the middle of the night. They find phrases from the Psalter on their lips at Mass. They interrupt their work in the fields or the workshops of the monastery to sing the Psalms of the day hours. They recite Psalms after their meals and practically the last words on their lips at night are verses written hundreds of years ago by one of the Psalmists.

For the monk who really enters into the full meaning of his vocation, the Psalms are the nourishment of his interior life and form the material of his meditations and of his own personal prayer, so that at last he comes to live them and experience them as if they were his own songs, his own prayers.

This would not be possible if the Psalms were nothing more than literature to those who have to pray them every day. "Art" and "literature" as such no doubt have a part to play in the monastic life. But when a man lives in the naked depths of an impoverished spirit, face to face with nothing but spiritual realities for year after year, art and literature can come to seem peculiarly shabby and unsubstantial—or else they become a lure and a temptation. In either case, they are a potential source of unrest and of dissatisfaction.

Yet the liturgical prayer of the monk is one of the great pacifying influences in a life that is all devoted to serenity and interior peace. There is only one explanation for this. The Psalms acquire, for those who know how to enter into them, a surprising depth, a marvelous and inexhaustible actuality. They are bread, miraculously provided by Christ, to feed those who have followed Him into the wilderness. I use this symbol advisedly. The miracle of the multiplication of the loaves usually suggests the Sacrament of the Eucharist, which it foreshadowed: but the reality which nourishes us in the Psalms is the same reality which nourishes us in the Eucharist, though

3

in a far different form. In either case, we are fed by the Word of God. In the Blessed Sacrament, " His flesh is food indeed." In the Scriptures, the Word is incarnate not in flesh but in human words. But man lives by every word that proceeds from the mouth of God.

This book is not a systematic treatise, but only a collection of personal notes on the Psalter. They are the notes of a monk, written in the monastic tradition, and one supposes that they might appeal above all to monks. But in this mysterious age, there is no telling whom the book may reach— although no one expects it to reach everybody. Perhaps, by its very nature, the book should pretend to address itself to those who do not quite understand why they are obliged, by reason of their vocation, to make the Psalms the substance of their prayer. In any case these pages attempt to put forth a few reasons why the Psalms in spite of their antiquity ought to be considered one of the most valid forms of prayer for men of all time. As for those readers who can only regard the Psalms as " literature"—this book will at least offer them some of the reasons why the Psalter seems to be more than literature to those of us who have made it our bread in the wilderness.

PSALMS AND CONTEMPLATION

I

1.

The Problem: Contemplation in the Liturgy

ST BENEDICT OF NURSIA, WRITING HIS RULE FOR
monks, was writing for men who have no other purpose in life but
God. After all, is there any other purpose for anyone? All men seek
God, whether they know it or not. As St Paul told the citizens of
Athens: "God, who made the world and all things therein . . . hath
made all mankind to dwell upon the whole face of the earth, deter-
mining appointed times and the limits of their habitation. That they
should seek God if haply they may feel after Him or find Him,
although He be not far from every one of us: For in Him we live
and move and have our being." [1] Even those who say they do not
believe in God, seek Him by the very fact that they deny Him: for
they would not deny Him unless they thought their denial were
true: and God is the source of all truth.

Among those who do believe in Him some seek Him more explicitly and more intently than others. Monks have no other occupation
in life than the search for God. That is what makes the monastic life
essentially simple. What could be simpler than the search for one
whom we have already found? That, indeed, is the nature of the
search: a realization that we have found Him. This realization begins
in an act of faith and culminates in an experience of His presence and
of His inscrutable and infinite identity, made known to us in the
descent of His mercy upon our souls which already exist only in Him
and by Him and for Him alone.

With this conception of the monastic life as a search for God in
which nothing is to be preferred to the love of Christ, St Benedict
never speaks in any but the simplest and most concrete terms. The
concrete realities of simple everyday human existence are nowhere
better appreciated than in a monastery where the monks, by their
"flight from the world," have actually found not only God but the
world also in Him. No one better than a monk realizes the dignity
and meaning of manual labor—not because labor is a penance, an
ascetical exercise, a means of livelihood or something else like that;
but because labor is itself worship, in a world which is sacrament-
alized by the presence of a creating and redeeming God.

Therefore, St Benedict does not deal in notions like "the Liturgical life," the "contemplative life," "infused contemplation."

Nor is he in any way concerned with a supposed theoretical opposition between "public official prayer" and "private prayer," between "vocal" and "mental prayer." He does not worry very much about the precise point at which contemplation ceases to be "acquired" and becomes "infused" — or whether two such categories actually exist. Such abstract matters have their place in modern theological dispute, but they were not very important to men who spent their lives not in arguing about "spirituality" but in loving God. This love led them to the knowledge which is true life, eternal life. "For this is eternal life, that they should know Thee the one true God and Jesus Christ whom Thou hast sent." [2]

These are the very reasons why the monks were true contemplatives, why they entered so deeply into that experience of the mysteries of God which is called "infused contemplation" and why, at the same time, they reached the end for which "liturgy" and the "liturgical life" have always been intended.

We, who are the descendants of St Benedict and who are often disturbed by some of the abstract questions I have mentioned, would do well to understand clearly, once and for all, that the neglect of theoretical dispute does not necessarily imply a neglect of the values which are being disputed. On the contrary the only way in which we can at last enter into the possession of these realities, which lie at the very roots of our monastic existence, is to stop talking about them and lay hands on them by living them out in the work of our contemplative vocation.

In saying that the Divine Office, the "work of God," held a central and dominant position in the monk's daily life, St Benedict was only reaffirming the truth that the monk came to the monastery to seek God. The term "opus Dei" (work of God), signifies the chanting of the canonical hours—the prayer of the monastic community. This choral office is made up above all of Psalms. But if we were to say that the chief purpose of the monk's life was the chanting of psalms we would certainly end up with a completely false notion of monasticism. It is not hard to see why. For if we define the monastic life merely in terms of the material obligation which the monk has to fulfil, we soon lose sight of the end which the legislator

I

PSALMS AND

CONTEMPLATION

has in view. The monk does not exist for the sake of an obligation: the obligation exists for the sake of the monk. Duties and obligations are merely the signposts which point out the road to some ultimate end in which our whole nature and its capacities are fulfilled. The fulfilment of an obligation does not, in itself, satisfy the aspirations of our being; but it brings us into contact with the One we seek. It unites us to God in a union of wills. And where the obligation is one of prayer, the union is more than a conformity of wills. Prayer demands intelligence. The Psalms bring our hearts and minds into the presence of the living God. They fill our minds with His Truth in order to unite us with His Love. Now there is a difference between praying and "saying prayers." I can, perhaps, exteriorly fulfil an obligation by "saying prayers"; but the reason for my being a monk is to *pray,* because in praying I find God.

The value of the work of God, the *opus Dei,* lies not so much in the fact that it is a work or a service *(opus),* but in the fact that it is service *of God.* Everything the monk does is done in the service of God. But the *opus Dei* is more perfectly and exclusively directed to God and penetrates more deeply into the deepest recesses of the monk's soul than any other thing he does. Of course, I am now taking liberties with St Benedict's term and extending it to include the Mass which is, in the strictest sense, our "Liturgy," and for which the office only forms a liturgical setting.

1. Contemplation in the Liturgy

That is why the *opus Dei* opens to us the deep springs of interior contemplation.

But we must not imagine that the chanting of psalms involves a "technique" of contemplation. The Psalms are not to be regarded as spiritual instruments, which, when they are properly manipulated, will lead us into some special psychological state. It is quite true that the tradition of the Fathers has always regarded "psalmody" as a step to "contemplation" and the Fathers always understood contemplation to be an *experience* of God. Since it is an experience, it clearly involves us in a psychological state, or at least in a psychological act. One of the Fathers of the Church who has the most to say about this contemplative experience is St Gregory the Great. And Gregory looms rather large in "liturgical spirituality" since

13

it is from him that the Gregorian Sacramentory and Gregorian chant take their names. I mention this in order to show that the mythical opposition between "liturgical prayer" and "contemplative experience" which gets some people so excited at the present day was unknown to the Fathers. For them "liturgy" and "contemplation" blended in a spontaneous harmony since both were expressions of the basic need for God and both contributed to the fulfilment of that need. For after all, "liturgy" turns into "contemplation" as soon as our prayer ceases to be a search for God and turns into a celebration, by interior experience, of the fact that we have found Him.

Nevertheless, I repeat, the psalms are not designed to "produce" contemplation. They are not, of themselves, supposed to induce any particular psychological effect. They lead to contemplation precisely because their impact on us is *theological* rather than *psychological*. There is no end of frustration in some monasteries where this truth has not been clearly understood. Neophytes in the contemplative life conceive that the "office" is an "obstacle to contemplative prayer" because it tends to prevent them from bringing upon themselves a certain degree of interior abstraction which is psychological in its origin and in its term. Their frustration is only increased, of course, when they are told by ascetics that the office is to be accepted merely as a form of penance. This amounts to a declaration that the Psalms have no meaning, that understanding has no place in prayer, that monastic choirs were invented only as a test of humility, abnegation and dogged endurance.

But the problem is not solved, either, by throwing the crumbs of David and Gregory to the monk's starved sense of art. The desire for contemplation has nothing essential to do with art or with the aesthetic sense. It cannot be satisfied by poetry, any more than it can by philosophy, or music, or ceremonies, or biblical speculation. After all, we will never come to contemplation unless we desire something infinitely more than contemplation. The Psalms, then, are not to be exploited for their psychological effects. These exist, but they are secondary. The psalms are theology. That means that they place us in direct contact with God, through the assent of faith to His Revelation. It is because of this theological and dynamic

I

PSALMS AND

CONTEMPLATION

effect that the psalms are steps to contemplation. This theological effect depends ultimately on a free gift of God. It is useless, then, to seek some secret esoteric "method" of reciting the Psalter in order to "get contemplation." If we chant the psalms with faith, God will manifest Himself to us; and that is contemplation.

2:

The Testimony of Tradition

THE MOVEMENT AWAY FROM SOCIAL AND LITURGICAL forms of prayer, which gained momentum in the high Middle Ages, made many Christians imagine that "interior" prayer "in spirit and in truth" was incompatible with exterior forms of worship. The Illuminists in sixteenth-century Spain taught their disciples that the chanting or recitation of the Divine Office was an obstacle to progress in interior prayer. Even some spiritual writers of a more orthodox stamp, who realized that the objective dignity and worth of the Divine Office as the public prayer of the Church, had to be defended and maintained, nevertheless treated it is a "duty" which the contemplative had to "accept" in all humility and submission, rather than as a manifestation of loving union with God.

Underlying this error was, first of all, a false psychology of contemplation. This false psychology was an oversimplification of the true doctrine. The false view went something like this. All contemplative prayer is purely passive prayer and is incompatible with any interior or exterior activity. The Divine Office involves exterior and interior activity. Therefore the Divine Office and contemplative prayer are incompatible.

The Quietist, Michael de Molinos, held that "interior (that is, contemplative) souls should never give thanks to God with words or with their tongue, but should remain in silence, placing no obstacle to His action in them." This sweeping statement was condemned. Molinos added (and this was also condemned) that the more perfectly these "interior" souls resigned themselves passively into the hands of God the more they would find it impossible to recite vocal prayers at all.

The reason heresies have to be condemned is that they contain elements that resemble the truth and therefore lead well-meaning Christians into error. It is quite true that in mystical or infused contemplation, the soul becomes increasingly passive under the guidance of the Holy Spirit, and it is also quite true that sometimes (but not *all the time*) the soul that is thus passively led by God finds it difficult or even impossible to elicit the various acts that enter into ordinary forms of prayer. But these passive states of prayer, which are a pure gift of God, are normally only granted by Him to souls who have faithfully exercised themselves in the practice of virtue and in the familiar types of meditative and vocal prayer. The road to this passivity is an active way, although that does not mean that passive prayer can be "acquired." That, in fact, was at the root of Molinos's errors. He believed that true contemplation could be acquired, in the strict sense of the word, by a mere cessation of activity. All you had to do was to renounce all prayer of petition, renounce all desire for virtue, for progress and for a supernatural reward, renounce all solicitude for your own body and soul, abandon all reflection on yourself and remain empty and passive in the hands of God and you automatically became a contemplative. This spiritual vacuum was itself contemplation because as soon as we ceased to act, God acted in us. It is easy to see why Molinos did not think vocal prayer was an aid to contemplation.

I

PSALMS AND

CONTEMPLATION

St Theresa, one of the best exponents of true mystical doctrine, seems to have been thinking of the Quietists when she wrote her *Way of Perfection*. She told the nuns of her first foundation, St Joseph's at Avila, that vocal prayer, well made, was necessarily also mental prayer, because if you did not apply your mind to what you were saying you were not — as far as she could see — praying at all. St Theresa was not here concerned with establishing the absolute minimum for satisfying an obligation in prayer. She had no hesitation in saying that vocal prayer, far from being an obstacle to contemplation, was one of the ordinary means by which we could dispose ourselves to receive this great gift of God. She said that "anyone ignorant of the subject" might imagine that vocal prayer and the (infused) prayer of quiet had nothing to do with each other, but that this was "certainly not true." [3] She went on to give examples of mystics who, in her own experience, had arrived at mystical union by the mere practice of vocal prayer. St Theresa herself believed and wrote that in the Pater Noster "Our Lord has taught us the whole method of prayer and high contemplation from the very beginnings of mental prayer, to quiet and union." [4]

When she said that the vocal prayers of the Church could lead us to the highest contemplation, St Theresa had centuries of tradition behind her. How else had the Fathers of the Desert found their way

18

into the regions of mystical prayer, save by the meditative recital of the Psalter? How else was the mysticism of a Gregory of Nyssa and a Cyril of Alexandria nourished but by the Liturgy, and above all by the Psalms? What prayer did more than the Divine Office to make mystics of the monks who once lived in great monastic communities like Jumièges, St Gall or Cluny, Calmaldoli or Clairvaux?

Wherever Catholics have lived as solitaries the claims of their solitude have always yielded at certain times to the demands of the *synaxis* — the assembly of the hermits in communal, liturgical prayer. The lives of the Desert Fathers show that the liturgical and sacramental life of the Church played an essential part in their contemplation. The *Historia Lausiaca* [5] gives us plenty of evidence that the test of false mysticism, among the hermits, was their attitude toward the Liturgy. Visionaries who came to believe that some private experience of the Absolute elevated them above the common sacramental life of the Church eventually proved — in ways as spectacular as they were disturbing, — that their interior life did not flow from springs divine. The reason for this is, of course, that there is no true mysticism without charity and there is no charity without incorporation in the Mystical Body of Christ, for charity is the life of that Mystical Body. But the life of the Mystical Body is nourished by the Sacraments and by the prayer of the Mystical Body, which is the Liturgy. The Desert Fathers who ran spiritually amok in the third and fourth centuries did not fail in asceticism. Their fasts and their penances were almost incredible. They were not without interior experiences: on the contrary, they often had the most spectacular visions. Where, then, did they fail? In humility and in charity. This failure was expressed in a contempt for mankind in general, for the other hermits, a contempt for the common prayer life of the Church and a conviction that they could do without Mass and the Sacraments. One of them even had a vision in which he believed that Christ appeared and told him he was now so perfect that he could do without the Holy Eucharist. He was too perfect to go to communion!

Cassian describes the Night Office of the Egyptian monks. They have come together by starlight and fill the shadows of the hut which is their chapel. How many are there? Cassian cannot tell. It takes him a long time to realize that the building is full of men, so great is the silence in which they stand, immobile, deep in recollection, while the solitary singer chants the Psalms in Coptic. . . The Office consists of twelve Psalms, chanted slowly. We can imagine the strange pathos of the Oriental melody, long since forgotten. Every one is intent upon the meaning of the Psalms, for the Desert Fathers, like the patriarchs and prophets of Israel, are haunted by the living reality of the Redeemer revealed to the world in the Psalter. He is the Word of God, hidden in these "words of God." Contemplation will come to them when the revelation that is given, in these inspired words, to the whole Church, suddenly opens out and becomes a personal experience, a deep, transforming, mystical light that penetrates and absorbs their whole being. That light, which is the fire of the Holy Spirit, will reach them through the Psalms. It is something far greater and more mysterious than the mere light of faith, and yet faith remains the key to it, for the way to contemplation is the way of faith. There is no other.

I

PSALMS AND

CONTEMPLATION

We must remember why the Desert Fathers lived the life they did. Their vocation—and this is the foundation stone of all monastic spirituality—had a twofold end. *Finis nostrae professionis regnum Dei. . . destinatio vero nostra, id est scopos, puritas est cordis.* "The ultimate end of our profession is the Kingdom of God . . . the proximate end, to which we direct our immediate strivings, is purity of heart." [6]

Everything the monk does then is ordered ultimately not only to his own fruition of God in heaven, but also to the transformation and glorification of all things in Christ, the "summing up of all things in Christ" which is the Kingdom of God. In order to achieve this last end, the monk directs his whole life to the acquisition of sanctity, purity of heart. *Puritas cordis* means much more to the Fathers than moral or even ascetic perfection. It is the end of a long process of spiritual transformation in which the soul, perfect in charity, detached from all created things, free from the movements of inordinate passion, is able to live absorbed in God, and is penetrated from time to time with vivid intuitions of His action, intuitions which plumb the depths of the divine mysteries, which "grasp" God in a secret and intimate experience not only of Who He is, but of what He is

20

doing in the world. The man who is pure in heart not only knows God, the Absolute Being, pure Act, but knows Him as the Father of Lights, the Father of Mercies, Who has so loved the world as to give His only begotten Son for its redemption. Such a man knows Him not merely by faith, not by theological speculation, but by intimate and incommunicable experience.

This purity of heart, which is the reason for the monk's existence since it perfects his union with God in experience and brings him to the gate of heaven, becomes the rule and measure of all his activities. Everything that brings him closer to this end is good. Everything that draws him away from the end is either useless or obnoxious. Things that are good in themselves may become harmful when the manner in which they are used turns them into obstacles to purity of heart. "It is necessary," said Abbot Isaac to Cassian in the desert, "that we carry out our exercises, fasts, vigils, prayers . . . for the sake of this end, purity of heart. But it is not fitting that we should disturb the order of this supreme virtue for the sake of our exercises. Indeed, if purity of heart is kept integral and untouched in our souls, nothing will be lost if, by necessity, we should have to pass over something that is secondary." [7]

The struggle for purity of heart goes through two phases: first the control of our actions and the acquisition of virtues and extinction of the passions. Then comes the more difficult part of the ascent: constant recollection of the mind in God. Cassian is often preoccupied with one of the great problems of monks: the problem of distractions. It is here that the meditation of Scripture and particularly the use of Scripture in liturgical and private prayer assumes a place of great importance.

The Egyptian monks memorized whole Books of the Bible. St Anthony, who is supposed not to have been able to read, meditated for years on the Scriptures in his solitude. He had learned them by heart from hearing them read and recited in the liturgical texts used in the churches. The words of Scripture are given to the monk first of all to drive out distracting and evil thoughts and replace them by good ones. We go to the Scriptures to find those "ascending" thoughts which raise us up to God against the gravitation of passion, in which "descending" thoughts constantly drag us earthward and tighten the chains which keep the spirit enslaved to the flesh. More than that, the meditation of the Scriptures leads to contemplation. Here Cassian strikes deep into the traditional doctrine which associates purity of heart with the restoration of the divine likenes to the soul, created in God's image but defaced by selfishness and sin.

You should show yourself diligent, indeed constant, in the reading of Scripture, until continual meditation fills your heart and forms you as it were after its likeness: while you make out of it in some way an ark of the covenant, having within you two tables of stone, which are the two testaments eternal and sure; and a golden pot that signifies a pure and sincere memory preserving with continual carefulness the manna hidden within it, the manna of everlasting and heavenly sweetness of the spiritual meaning and the bread of angels: the rod of Aaron, too, which represents the saving standard of our supreme and true High Priest, Jesus Christ, which for ever buds with the freshness of immortal memory . . . All these are guarded by two Cherubim, the fulness of historical and spiritual knowledge. [8]

Cassian goes on to elaborate this symbolism—which he does in perfect accord with a tradition dating back to the Apostles—by explaining that the "spiritual knowledge" of Scripture, like the Cherubs which overshadowed the Ark in the Holy of Holies, protects and overshadows the inner sanctuary of the soul. This knowledge of Scripture is not contemplation. It leads to contemplation. It preserves the atmosphere necessary for contemplation. It is the bulwark of purity of heart. It protects the soul against movements of passion, against the temptations of the evil spirits. Overshadowed by the spiritual understanding of Scripture, the soul, gathered in silent recollection in its own depths, adores the Living God Who is present there. "Thus" says Cassian, "the soul advances not only into the ark of the Covenant but into the priestly kingdom, and there, with a love unchanging in its purity, absorbed in contemplative prayer *(spiritualibus disciplinis)*, it fulfils the office of the High Priest who is commanded in the Law not to come out of the holy of holies . . . which is his own heart, where God promises to dwell at all times, saying 'I will dwell in them and walk among them.' " [9]

Over and over again in the Fourteenth Conference, on the spiritual understanding of Scripture, Cassian keeps telling us that this understanding goes hand in hand with purity of heart and with true contemplation. The Spiritual Master who attempts to teach this understanding of the Scriptures without having experienced it himself only multiplies vain words, learned though they may be. It is true that worldly, impure and proud men seem to possess this knowledge of the Scriptures, but it is a false science, a combination of rhetorical skill and academic subtleties. The Psalms, says Cassian, teach us the true path to the spiritual understanding of Scripture: the path of active purification and of meditation on the Law. When the Psalmist says that only those who are "undefiled in the way" can arrive at a spiritual understanding of the Law of God, he is saying that no one can reach this end "unless he travel without fault in the way of Christ." We shall see later what the Fathers meant by the spiritual understanding of the Law.

This spiritual understanding of Scripture is acquired after meditation of the Scriptures in the silence of the night, and in solitude. But the fruit of the monk's private meditations is tasted in the recitation of the Psalms in choir. In order to preserve the contemplative character of the office, the number of Psalms was restricted to twelve and in between Psalms the monks prostrated themselves on the ground for brief periods of silent interior prayer. The "office" was deliberately kept simple, without ornament, without useless accretions, and the monks resisted the temptation to pile litanies upon litanies and prayers upon prayers, substituting quantity for quality. *Non enim multitudine versuum sed mentis intelligentia delectantur.* [10] "They do not delight in the number of verses they recite but in the spiritual understanding with which they recite them." And he goes on, "They hold it to be of greater importance to recite ten verses in an intelligent and orderly fashion than to rush through a whole Psalm in confusion of mind."

In the Ninth Conference, on prayer, Cassian goes into details about pure prayer and the need for detachment and interior recollection. He discusses the ordinary degrees of prayer. He gives a short commentary on the Our Father, the model of all prayer, and then turns to contemplative prayer, to which we are drawn if we make good use of vocal prayers and especially of the Our Father. This contemplative prayer has various degrees. Prayer is pure and perfect, according to the authority of St Anthony, when the contemplative no longer realizes that he is praying or indeed that he exists at all. [11]

A lower degree of contemplation is one in which the effects of grace are more positively felt. Cassian has a picturesque name for it. He calls it the "Prayer of Fire." It is the sort of prayer that characterises the flamelike movements of spiritual understanding stirred by the finger of God in the heart of the monk chanting the Psalms in recollection, with deep compunction, and with a sudden poignant realization of the concrete, intimate reality of the mercy of God, of the presence of Christ, of union with God, through Christ, in the Holy Spirit!

Cassian believed that this kind of spiritual understanding was supposed to be the ordinary fruit of vocal prayer, choral prayer, and of the Our Father. He interprets the Gospel references to Christ praying alone on the mountain, or in the Garden of the Agony, as implicit counsels of the Savior urging His followers to aspire to this perfect prayer. Yet the "Prayer of Fire," he says, "is known to few."

Soaring above every human sense, it is uttered not by the sound of the voice nor by the movement of the tongue nor by any formation of words. Filled and illumined with light from heaven, the mind does not utter this prayer in limited and human expressions, but with all its powers gathered together in unity it pours forth this prayer abundantly as from a most copious fountain and offers it up to God in a way beyond expression, telling Him so much in that brief moment of time that when we return to ourselves afterwards we are not able easily to state or even to go over in our minds all that took place. [12]

I

PSALMS AND

CONTEMPLATION

3:

Meanings in Scripture

MANY OF THE PSALMS SEEM TO HAVE LITTLE OR nothing to do with contemplation. What do Og the King of Basan and Sehon the King of the Amhorrites have to offer the contemplative soul, the *anima sitiens Deum?* [13] In many of the Psalms we seem to be incited to thirst not for God but for the blood of our enemies. We sometimes are invited to relax, not so much in the obscure experience of a merciful and loving Presence, as in the neolithic satisfaction with which " the just man shall wash his hands in the blood of a sinner." When we are not joining in the war-cry of a race of savages, perhaps we are considering the history of that race's barbarity, its superstitions, lusts, its treacheries without number, all the prevarications that called down upon it the vengeance of a jealous God. Are we supposed to enter into the prayer of fire as we travel through a "land polluted with blood" in which the Children of Israel are engaged in sacrificing their sons and daughters to devils? [14]

The case against the Psalter would be devastating if we assumed that the Psalms were supposed to contain a system of precepts and techniques for the interior life like for instance the *Baghavad Gita*. Taking the Psalter as a whole, and in its relation to the rest of the Old Testament, we find that the spiritual wisdom contained in it is something quite different from anything to be found in the writings of pagan philosophers and mystics. Only a few of the Psalms are didactic in the ordinary sense of that word. And even when the Psalms do give us ethical precepts, these appear to be rather prosaic and down to earth in their practicality. " Blessed the man who follows not the counsel of the ungodly, And enters not into the way of sinners, and sits not in the company of the insolent; But his delight is in the law of the Lord, and on his law he ponders day and night. And he is like a tree planted by running waters, That yields its fruit in due season, and whose leaves wither not, and whatsoever he does, prospers." [15] The Psalms themselves later on have to face the unpleasant question presented by the fact that the just man does not, in fact, always prosper. His leaf does fall off and he does not bear fruit, while the storehouses of the wicked are full, their sheep fruitful, their oxen fat and their daughters go about in jewels, as the Vulgate has it, " sculptured like pillars of the temple." [16]

27

Yet although the literal meaning of the Psalter is sometimes glorious, sometimes bloody and sometimes simply sensible and prosaic the Psalms have, in fact, always formed contemplatives since the first days of the Church, and they have provided the constant basic spiritual nourishment of Catholic mysticism, along with the rest of Scripture. The Fathers of the Church and the contemplative saints, aware that their deepest experience of God was always somehow associated with the Liturgy and intimately dependent on the Psalms, have sometimes proceeded to argue, *a posteriori*, that the true meaning of the Psalms was a hidden and allegorical meaning. This is what has sometimes been called the "mystical" sense of Scripture. The literal sense, with its battles, its triumphs, its agonies and its moralizing, is only an outer shell. The "real" meaning of the Psalms is held to be a spiritual kernel which must be arrived at by penetration of the "letter." To cling to the literal meaning alone is, according to this line of thought, to miss the whole significance of the Psalms, for "the letter killeth."

A Catholic contemplative instinctively seeks something more than the testimony of individual mystics and saints about their experience of God. Catholic contemplation is essentially founded on dogmatic truth. It is more than a quest for the Absolute which can be satisfied by appropriate techniques of recollection. The Catholic mystic seeks, above all, the mind and truth of God. And he seeks it in the word of God. If he withdraws from the world and stands at the frontiers of eternity, it is because he somehow hopes to see God, or at least to hear His voice. If he calls out to God in prayer, it is because he desires an answer. And the answer he desires is not merely the voice of his own fancy, or the echo of another human experience like his own. It must be God's answer.

The Church urges us to seek above all the *theology* that is revealed to us in Scripture. The true function of scriptural interpretation is to make clear the Truths that God has revealed to us about Himself and about His action in time and in human history. It is this above all that the contemplative will seek. It cannot be found without a healthy respect for the literal sense of the Bible. But all the other senses will have a certain importance.

I do not intend to enter into a technical discussion of the various senses of Scripture here. The terminology itself would be infinitely confusing. It is enough to say that there are two senses in Scripture that are really vitally important for the contemplative. These are the *literal* sense of Scripture, which is the meaning of the words of the text, and the *typical* sense of Scripture which is the meaning of events narrated in the text. All the other senses of Scripture that have any theological value can be reduced to these two.

The miracle of the brazen serpent is recorded in the *Book of Numbers*. The literal sense of the passage simply records the miracle. It tells us what took place. The Children of Israel were complaining of the hardships they suffered in the Arabian desert. As a punishment for their complaints, they became the victims of " fiery serpents " which bit them and killed many. This brought about a prompt change of heart, and the people begged Moses to intercede for them and get rid of these snakes. At the command of God, Moses made a brazen serpent, and set it up for a sign and everyone who looked upon the sign was cured of his snake-bite. So much for the letter. But the event itself has a symbolic significance. It contains within itself a hidden truth, it points to another event. It is intended by God to signify this other reality. The miracle of Moses is called a " type " and the reality it signifies is called its " antitype ". The full theological import of the miracle of the brazen serpent does not become clear to us until we see the type fulfilled in its antitype.

3. Meanings in Scripture

But who is to tell us the typical sense of any given passage of Scripture? God alone. Why? Because the typical sense of Scripture is a hidden sense, known only to the author of Scripture, who is God. Therefore if we are to find out the typical sense of any part of Scripture we must consult the Author of Scripture. How? In His revelation. That is to say that if the types in the Old Testament are to be made clear to us in their antitypes, this clarification must come from God Himself, either in some other passage of Scripture or in some other fount of revelation.

In the case of the brazen serpent there is no difficulty, because Jesus himself explained to Nicodemus that " as Moses lifted up the brazen serpent in the desert, so must the Son of Man be lifted up:

that whosoever believeth in Him may not perish, but may have life everlasting.''[17] The Mystery hidden in the miracle of the brazen serpent is the Mystery of the Cross.

The Christian contemplative therefore can use this passage of the *Book of Numbers* just as well as any passage in the New Testament as a fruitful subject of meditation. Indeed, this mysterious "typology" which everywhere compenetrates the Old Testament and New, accounts in large part for the contemplation the Fathers and Saints of the Church were able to draw from the Divine Office.

Now we must never confuse "typology" and "allegory." The typical sense of Scripture is not allegorical. In allegory there is only one reality, signified in improper terms. In typology there are two realities, one signifying the other. The abuse of Scriptural allegory in the Middle Ages has left a certain mark of opprobrium on the spiritual interpretation of the Bible. Some theologians, failing to make the proper distinctions, still believe that the "typical" sense of Scripture is to be distrusted. One of the characteristics of Counter-Reformation Catholic theology was a reaction against allegory and against a too independent interpretation of the Scriptures, in favor of the liturgical and critical study of the sacred texts. At the same time, the trend of modern thought away from symbolism has frustrated the basic human need for symbol and metaphor to the point of perversion: we have become instinctively suspicious of that for which we are starved. A world without imagination, which is no longer able to cope with the immaterial and which is incapable of the simplest efforts to link two terms of an analogy, condemns all symbolism as mystification. A superficial glance at the Scriptural allegories of some of the Fathers, or, for that matter, of the Talmud and the *midrashim,* is enough to confirm these suspicions beyond hope of appeal. The "spiritual sense" of Scripture has, in fact, been stretched at times to excessive lengths. Often it has had no serious foundation in the despised "letter." Obviously, a mystery that is drawn forth from what the letter does not say cannot be regarded as divine revelation. It comes not from God but from the exegete's own imagination. Very often,

I

PSALMS AND

CONTEMPLATION

too, the extension of the spiritual sense has been over-estimated. Only a few texts in the Bible are clearly capable of a mystical interpretation.

The Jews had already developed an allegorical interpretation of the Old Testament before the Fathers of the Church began to produce systematic "mystical" commentaries along the lines of the Jewish *Midrashim*. The Jewish contemplative, Philo of Alexandria, paved the way for Origen, St Gregory of Nyssa, and for a long line of Christian exegetes. At the same time, the Gnostics had been interpreting the Old Testament in a figurative sense and their ideas were later taken up by the Manichaeans. Christian spiritual exegesis began to appear first of all in fragmentary fashion, in controversy against the Jews, Gnostics and other sects. It was the task of the Christian apologists of the second and third centuries to prove, against the Gnostics, that the two Testaments formed an organic unity and, against the Jews, that the Old Testament was incomplete and indeed incomprehensible without its fulfilment in the New. Proofs of this were found in the fulfilment of literal messianic prophecies and confirmed elsewhere by mystical "figures" or "types."

The discovery of these types in the Old Testament had characterized the exegesis of the Apostles and of Christ Himself, and we find the typical sense of the Old Testament affirmed everywhere in the New. Indeed, the first words uttered by St Peter on Pentecost when the Church, visibly filled with the fire of the Holy Ghost, first began to speak for herself, were an assertion of the fulfilment of the whole Old Testament in the death and resurrection of Jesus and the formation of the Church. St Peter told the Jews, who had gathered in Jerusalem from all parts of the world and who wondered at the fact that the Galilean disciples of Christ were speaking all the languages of the earth, that this very fact was a fulfilment of a messianic utterance of the prophet Joel. "It shall come to pass in the last days, (saith the Lord,) I will pour out my Spirit upon all flesh...." The expression, "the last days" refers of course to the definitive establishment of the messianic kingdom, everywhere foretold in the Old Testament.

St Peter had no need to appeal to any hidden "figure" in the text he quoted from Joel. The charisms Joel had referred to were evidently verified. The Spirit had been poured out. The literal sense of the prophecy was plainly fulfilled before their eyes. But then St Peter went on from this to argue that if the Kingdom had come, if the "last days," "the fulness of time" had now arrived, it must be because Jesus was the Messias. And in fact, Jesus Whom they had crucified had risen from the dead. He was the Son of God. It was His to pour out the Spirit of God upon the earth. All this, Peter reasoned, had been foretold of Christ in the Psalms. And here we come to the truly spiritual sense of Scripture. In the Psalms David speaks as if he were not to die, as if God were not to "leave him in hell" or allow him to "see corruption." God was to raise up David, and make him sit at His right hand. And yet David was dead. David had not risen, nor had he ascended into heaven and his Kingdom had vanished from the earth. What was all this about victory over death, and about an everlasting Kingdom?

I

PSALMS AND

CONTEMPLATION

"Ye men, brethren," said St Peter," let me freely speak to you of the Patriarch David; that he died and was buried : and his sepulchre is with us to the present day. Whereas therefore he was a prophet and knew that God hath sworn to him with an oath that of the fruit of his loins one should sit upon his throne. Foreseeing this, he spoke of the resurrection of Christ. For neither was he left in hell, neither did his flesh see corruption." [18]

The Psalms were seen by the Apostles to be the utterances not only of David but of the future Christ. God Himself, Who spoke in David and Who was to become incarnate as the "Son of David," was speaking of His own coming as the Christ. The "mystical" sense of Scripture shows us everywhere God gradually manifesting Himself in the world, manifesting not only His Divine Nature and attributes but also His plan for the salvation of men. The plan is finally made known in its fulfilment. It is only fully understood by those *in whom it is fulfilled*.

Origen and the exegetical School of Alexandria developed the spiritual interpretation of Scripture to a high degree of perfection and the influence of Origen was to extend down through the Christian

Middle Ages in spite of the reaction of the School of Antioch. This school was somewhat suspicious of the freedom with which the "mystical" interpretation handled the Scriptures, and it returned to a more cautious emphasis on the "letter."

One of the interesting implications of Origen's distinction between the "letter" and the "spirit" was the fact that the "spiritual sense" laid open its secrets only to those who were advanced, perfect in the spiritual life. It was therefore closely associated with sanctity and with *gnosis*—contemplation. The lavish use of Old Testament texts in a typological sense by the Church in her liturgy tended to confirm the Origenist tendency, without sanctioning all its exaggerations. At the same time, the Antiochian suspicion of the "spiritual sense" finally brought upon itself an open condemnation of extreme literalism in the interpretation of Scripture. Theodore of Mopsuestia, who had commented on the Psalms and reduced the number of messianic "types" in the Psalter to an absolute minimum, was condemned by the second Council of Constantinople. Mopsuestus had maintained that only seven of the Psalms were messianic. Four were messianic in the literal sense and three in the typical sense. The real reason for his condemnation was his Nestorianism, of which this exegetical error was only a result and an expression.

It is interesting to notice that the merits of the spiritual and literal senses of Scripture are being debated today with almost as much heat as they were in the third and fourth centuries—although perhaps the debate does not affect quite so many people, since it can be carried on without political repercussions!

Paul Claudel, for instance, has come out as an ardent champion of the "spiritual" sense of the Scriptures and has himself commented on some of the books of the Old Testament—Ruth, the Canticle of Canticles, and so on—making a rather free and individual use of the old "allegorical" tradition. Claudel's commentaries have a value that is literary rather than exegetical. They make good reading, and they do us the service of recognizing the *poetic* character of poetic books. But that does not mean that Claudel's beautiful intuitions into the poetic value of the text necessarily always penetrate to the real meaning of the inspired writer. Paul Claudel has simply rebelled

33

against the stupidity and bad taste of a passing generation of commentators who have had a peculiar talent for burying essentials under useless details. What is the good of an erudition so short-sighted that it cannot even recognize the literary character of the book which it pretends to be studying? Can a poem be understood when it is treated merely as an archeological document? Yet when the poem is, in fact, ancient, we need more than the connatural affinity of poetic taste to get at its real meaning.

Other interpreters of Scripture have gone too far in their reaction against rationalism and higher criticism. They have come out with an assertion that certain exegetical problems can only be solved by an appeal to a hidden, spiritual meaning, without any need for scientific scrutiny of the letter. The Holy See, which is driving ahead with full force toward a new critical edition of the Bible and which encourages every form of scientific study of the Scriptures has condemned this futile expedient.

At the same time, Pius XII, in his Encyclical *Divino Afflante Spiritu,* has called our attention to the right use of the spiritual sense of Scripture and has once more urged interpreters of the Bible to return to the Fathers and make use of their labors in this matter. The most important task of the Scripture scholar, Pius XII says, is to discover and to expound the real meaning of the books which the Church believes to have God for their Author. The study of ancient languages, of biblical archeology and history, the use of all the modern critical apparatus which explores the texts and versions of the Bible, has only one end : to lead us to a deeper and more accurate understanding of what God has revealed, for our salvation. The chief task of the exegete is, of course, to discover the literal sense of the Scriptures. Without that, "typology" would be a pure illusion. Nevertheless, the Holy Father regrets the fact that so many commentaries have applied themselves almost exclusively to matters belonging to "the historical, philological and other auxiliary sciences." The Church desires above all that the full content of revelation be made known, and this in such a way that it may be accessible to everyone. Now the full theological meaning of the Bible, as Pius XII clearly indicates in the encyclical we are discussing, is not arrived at without an under-

I

PSALMS AND

CONTEMPLATION

standing of the spiritual sense. Even though the letter of Scripture contains in itself enough to nourish a deep interior life, we must also understand the spiritual sense, and here Pius XII gives a simple description of what the "mystical" sense of Scripture really is:

What was done and said in the Old Testament was ordained and disposed by God with such consummate wisdom that things past prefigured in a spiritual way those that were to come under the new dispensation of grace. Wherefore the exegete, just as he must search out and expound the literal meaning of the words intended and expressed by the sacred writer, so also must he do likewise for the spiritual sense, provided it is clearly intended by God. For God alone could have known this spiritual meaning and could have revealed it to us. Now our Divine Saviour Himself points out to us and teaches this same sense in the Holy Gospel; the Apostles also, following the example of the Master, profess it in their spoken and written words; the unchanging tradition of the Church approves it; finally the most ancient usage of the liturgy proclaims it, wherever may be rightly applied the well-known principle, The rule of prayer is the rule of faith. Let Catholic exegetes then disclose and expound this spiritual significance, intended and ordained by God, with that care which the dignity of the divine word demands; but let them scrupulously refrain from proposing as the genuine meaning of Sacred Scripture other figurative senses. [19]

An important aspect of the mystical sense of Scriptures was developed by the Fathers of the Alexandrian school. This was the application of the figures of the Old Testament to the interior life of the soul in whom the Kingdom of God has come through the charity, poured out by the Spirit sent by Christ. According to this moral sense already indicated in the Epistles of St. Paul, the realities externally fulfilled in the Mystery of Christ are also fulfilled at the same time, in their own appropriate way, in the souls of those who have entered into that mystery and whose life is Christ.

The writers of the New Testament everywhere assert that the *pascha Christi*, the descent of the Word of God into the world, His death on the Cross, His resurrection and ascent into heaven, opening heaven to the sons of men, is the fulfilment of the "type" which was the exodus of the Jews out of Egypt. Already the prophets of the Old Testament had seen in this exodus a prophecy of the return of the Jews from that other captivity, in Babylon. The Christians themselves saw the return from Babylon to Jerusalem as a type of the messianic kingdom, the establishment of the Church. After all, was not Jerusalem destroyed, and were not the Jews scattered to the ends of the earth? One might well argue, in the same way, that the Church herself has always been subject to attack and is never too secure in this world. But the Church herself looks ahead to a final and definitive fulfilment of the "Exodus" when all the redeemed shall ascend in glory to heaven and time shall be no more.

Meanwhile, we are passing through the desert on our way to the promised land.

Now what is already fulfilled in Christ, in the Church and in her sacraments, finds its realization in each individual soul who, by the sacraments, enters upon and lives the "mystery of Christ," the *pascha Christi*. Hence the spiritual interpretation of Scripture discovers an evident continuity between the first born of the Jews spared by the exterminating angel because of the blood of the paschal lamb, Jesus the first born of a new humanity, conquering death by His own blood, and finally the Christian, marked by the Blood of this true Lamb of God in the sacrament of baptism which "buries him in the death of Christ." [20] The univocal character of grace in the old law and the new—since all grace and all sanctification come from Christ—guarantees an essential likeness between the experience of the chosen people in the desert, the experience of the prophets who not only foretold Christ but prefigured Him, the experience of Christ Himself, and finally the experience of the saints mystically united to Christ. All these are the work of one Spirit who reveals to us in Scripture His pattern, His mode of action and the fulfilment of His plan. In those who accept the "word of the Cross" that is preached to them, the same Holy Spirit begins at once to work the mystery of the Cross. The initial act of faith which admits us, by grace, into the divine mysteries foreshadowed and worked out in the Scriptures, reproduces in us the death of Christ and His resurrection from the dead. Even from the psychological viewpoint the act of faith is like a passage through the Red Sea and a journey, nourished by miraculous food, through the blighted heart of a land without

I

PSALMS AND
CONTEMPLATION

vegetation. As we grow in faith, the mystery of Exodus, and the *pascha Christi* tend to become more and more a matter of experience in our lives. Nevertheless the experience itself is not the important thing : it is only the accidental effect of a deeper theological reality, and this reality is infinitely beyond experience, *it is God Himself in us.*

Ultimately, the spiritual understanding of Scripture leads to a mystical awareness of the Spirit of God Himself living and working in our own souls, carrying out, by His mysterious power, in our own lives, the same salvific actions which we can see prefigured and then realized in the Old and New Testaments. This was the profound truth on which St John of the Cross could base his whole mystical theology, which, as we have shown elsewhere, is entirely centered in and dependent upon the mystery of Christ. [21]

But it must be remembered that this experience itself is only accessory and accidental. The substantial reality of our spiritual life is nourished and maintained by faith, hope and love through the instrumentality of the Seven Sacraments. These Sacraments are the prolongation, in the New Law, of the " mighty works of God " in the Old. The whole sacramental and liturgical life of the Church not only contemplates the wonders of God in the Old Testament, not only comments on them, explains them, re-enacts them but actually lives them and fulfils them.

The Church is made up of living individual men. It is a kind of " mystical person " composed of many persons who are one in Christ and who share His own divine life. The mystical sense of Scripture is then not merely something which the Church *studies* but something which the Church *lives* and *is*. But this cannot be so unless we, who are the Church, experience in our lives the mystery of Christ. That is why the Liturgy would have us constantly go back to the beginning and work our way down to what we are through the types and figures which foreshadowed the whole Christ, the Head and the Members, the Jesus Who died on Calvary and Who lives in us, Who dies in us that others may live in Him.

The fruitful use of the Liturgy then can be summed up in this experience of the Mystery of Christ. Liturgical prayer does not endeavor to raise us up to something we are not : it reminds us that we have already been to some extent transformed : it assures us that the beginnings of transformation are a pledge and foreshadowing of its completion. The spiritual understanding of the Psalter will therefore not introduce us to some esoteric technique of prayer, nor will it tempt us to induce within our minds some peculiar psychological state. It will, above all, tell us not merely what we ought to be but the unbelievable thing that we already *are*. It will tell us over and over again that we are Christ in this world, and that He lives in us, and that what was said of Him has been and is being fulfilled in us: and that the last, most perfect fulfilment of all is now, at this moment, by the theological virtue of hope, placed in our hands. Thus the liturgy of earth is necessarily one with the liturgy of heaven. We are at the same time in the desert and in the Promised Land. The Psalms are our Bread of Heaven in the wilderness of our Exodus.

I

PSALMS AND

CONTEMPLATION

4:

Songs of the City of God

WE HAVE ONLY ONE MASTER OF THE SPIRITUAL
life, one Master in the ways of prayer: Christ. *Unus est Magister
Vester, Christus.* The Church, the Mystical Body of Christ, continues
His teaching and sanctifying office among us. She has the aim, obligation and function of bringing all men to the knowledge, love
and contemplation of God and of "restoring all things in Christ"
Who, is the light of the world. The Church is therefore entrusted
with the greatest of all functions: that of fulfilling the whole purpose of God in creating the universe and in creating man. The
whole meaning of human existence is in the hands of the Church,
man's fate depends on her Sacraments, her Liturgy and her priesthood. But the teaching and sanctifying power of the Church are
inseparable from her jurisdiction. She teaches and administers the
Sacraments by virtue of an authority divinely committed to her,
and she has the power to support her teaching and her ritual with
doctrinal pronouncements and disciplinary decrees.

If we are ever to become contemplatives, we must be formed,
remotely or more directly, by all these. The Church and no other
can rightly direct and dispose us to mystical prayer. She it is who
must guide us in our understanding of Scripture as well as in our
use of the inspired text for our liturgical prayer. But at the same
time it is she who protects us in our interior liberty, defends us
against the tyranny of restricted human systems and "schools of
spirituality" that might tend to narrow us down to a particular
esoteric outlook and leave us something less than Catholics.

Her Liturgy is at once a safe and universal school of contemplation. Why? Because the Church is guided by the Spirit of
God Who embraces all in His infinite simplicity. The Holy Ghost is
her life and He is also the source and mover of her prayer. The Holy
Ghost prays in the Liturgy and when we pray with the Liturgy the
Holy Ghost, the Spirit of Christ, prays in us. He teaches us how to
pray by praying in us. He not only gives us words to say and sing, He
also sings them in our hearts. And when, as must inevitably happen,
we fall far short of understanding or appreciating what the prayers
mean, the Spirit of God "helps our weakness," asking on our behalf,
with a fervor of infinite love we shall never be able to comprehend.

I

PSALMS AND

CONTEMPLATION

"The things that are of God no man knoweth, but the Spirit of God," says St Paul. "Now we have received not the spirit of this world but the Spirit that is of God that we may know the things that are given us from God."[22] This text tells us quite evidently not only that all our contemplation is a work produced in us by the Holy Spirit, but also that the Holy Ghost teaches us contemplation in the Scriptures which He Himself inspired, because the revealed word of God is one of the most important of "the things that are given us from God." It is the Holy Ghost, then, who will lead us to contemplation by opening to us the depths of meaning hidden in the Psalms. We have received this Holy Spirit in Baptism. Our progress in the supernatural life, which is also the life of interior prayer, normally means a progressive *revelation* of God, to us, in our souls and in all His gifts to us.

The Mass, which is the central Mystery of the whole Christian economy, since it is the Sacrifice in which Christ offers Himself to the Father for the sins of the world, is the center of the Liturgy. But by means of the Sacraments, Sacramentals and above all of the Divine Office, the Church seeks to vivify every moment of the Christian's day and every department of his life with the streams of grace and truth which flow into our souls from Christ's Cross. Pope Pius XII, in his Encyclical on the Liturgy [23] speaks of this great work of sanctification in terms which suggest, to anyone familiar with Christian mystical tradition, that contemplation is the normal fulfilment of the liturgical life, for he says: "The ideal of the Christian life is that each one be united to God in the closest and most intimate manner." The Holy Father continues:

For this reason the worship that the Church renders to God and which is based especially on the Eucharistic Sacrifice and the use of the Sacraments, is directed and arranged in such a way that it embraces, by means of the Divine Office, the hours of the day, the weeks and the whole cycle of the year, and reaches all the aspects and phases of human life. [24]

In the same encyclical, Pope Pius XII describes the interior activity of a soul engaged in liturgical prayer, showing how an active participation in the Liturgy brings about union with God. He says:

It is not merely a question of recitation or of singing which, however

42

perfect according to the norms of music and the sacred rites only reaches the ear, but it is especially a question of the ascent of the mind and the heart to God so that, united with Christ, we may completely dedicate ourselves and all our actions to Him.

For the Psalms to fulfil the function Christian tradition has always demanded of them, which is to dispose the souls of men for union with God, they must not only "raise the minds and hearts of men to God" but they must inspire us to give ourselves entirely to God. Finally, most important of all, this gift of ourselves must be made in Christ and with Christ. Our sacrifices have no supernatural value except in so far as they are united with the One Sacrifice which alone is acceptable to God and infinitely pleasing in His sight.

There is a contemplation proper to the metaphysician, in which the mind of man can rest in a pure but abstractive intuition of an "Infinite Being." This is not what Christianity means by "raising the mind and heart to God." Christianity is not content with finding God in His immanence—as He is present in the metaphysical depths of everything that is—it also seeks Him in His infinite transcendence. 4. *Songs of the City of God* He is so far above all being that He cannot be said to "be" in the same sense as contingent beings. No system of asceticism, no mystical cult, however esoteric, however pure, can suffice to bridge the abyss between us and this Transcendent Creator of all being. And yet He is our Creator and our Father, and we can speak to Him and hear Him answer us. How? Because He has revealed Himself to us in our own language and has given us human words in which to praise and pray to Him. More than that, He descends into our sphere and takes part in our own life. He has manifested Himself not only in creation, not only in revelation, but in the divine and mysterious acts by which He has entered into human history and appropriated it to Himself, so that Christ's Cross has become the key to a history whose purpose is to separate the City of God from the city of this world, which has Babylon for its symbolic name.

The Psalms are the songs of this City of God. They are therefore the voice of the Mystical Body of Christ. They are the songs of Christ. They are the songs of God in this world. Singing them, we become more fully incorporated into the mystery of God's action in human history.

Pope Pius XII emphasizes this traditional Catholic doctrine in his *Mediator Dei*:

By assuming human nature, the Divine Word introduced into this exile a hymn which is sung in heaven for all eternity. He unites to Himself the whole human race and with it sings this hymn of praise to God.

In this same passage, the Holy Father illustrates his statement with a quotation from St Augustine's commentary on the Psalms. No theologian has ever set forth the doctrine of the Mystical Body of Christ with such clarity and in such detail as St Augustine who is, in every respect, the most Catholic of the Fathers, for his theological horizons are never narrowed down to anything less comprehensive than the " Whole Christ." Not only in his *City of God,* but precisely in his exegesis of the Psalms, St Augustine lays open to us the Mystery of our union with God in Christ. There above all he shows us that the Liturgy is the voice of Christ.

What could be more evident than the words of Pius X in his *Motu Proprio* of 1903? In contemplation, as in everything else that is Christian, "the Liturgy is the primary and indispensable source of the genuine Christian spirit."

I

PSALMS AND

CONTEMPLATION

5:

Errors to Avoid

IF A CONTEMPLATIVE WERE TO REGARD THE Mass and Office as secondary in his interior life, he would run a serious risk of coming to a standstill in his prayer, and even of falling into illusion. But here a distinction must be made. It must be admitted that the individual vocation to contemplative prayer is conditioned by individual temperament, and that there will always be souls who will usually find a deeper conscious peace and absorption in the presence of God when they are silent and alone than when they are praying in choir. Generally speaking—and here we follow the authority of St John of the Cross—the soul called by God to infused contemplation is by that very fact called to a state of " restful tranquillity in which it is abundantly infused with the spirit of Divine wisdom, which is the loving, tranquil, lonely, peaceful, sweet, inebriator of the spirit. Hereby the soul feels itself to be gently and tenderly wounded and ravished, knowing not by whom, nor whence, nor how."[25]

It is important for such souls to realize that the graces of the Office actually nourish and stimulate this solitary contemplation. After chanting the Psalms in choir they will be more surely and sweetly drawn than ever, to this intimate absorption in God and the more fervent they have been in the chanting of God's praises in choir, the greater fruit will they draw, as a result, from the silent communion in which the Holy Spirit inspires them to prolong their prayer after the Office has ended. St Benedict did not expect all his monks to receive such graces but he explicitly legislated to protect those who did, and to keep them from being distracted by their more active brethren. [26]

The heart of contemplative prayer is a selflessness that assimilates the soul to God and enables it to receive those supernatural "touches" of grace by which it becomes aware of God, as He is in Himself, not through the medium of ideas and species, which cannot perfectly represent Him as He is in Himself, but in the immediate contact of obscure love. The secret of contemplation is the gift of ourselves to God. This, too, is the secret of the Psalter. God will give Himself to us through the Psalter if we give ourselves to Him without reserve, in our recitation of the Psalms. This implies three things : a pure faith and an intense desire of love and above all a firm hope of finding God hidden in His revealed word. To say this is only to say that the worthy chanting of the Divine Office involves a constant and perfect exercise of the theological virtues which are the only path to contemplative prayer.

I

PSALMS AND

CONTEMPLATION

POETRY SYMBOLISM & TYPOLOGY

II

Poetry, Symbolism & Typology

THE PSALMS ARE POEMS, AND POEMS HAVE A
meaning—although the poet has no obligation to make his meaning
immediately clear to anyone who does not want to make an effort
to discover it. But to say that poems have meaning is not to say that
they must necessarily convey practical information or an explicit
message. In poetry, words are charged with meaning in a far different way than are the words in a piece of scientific prose. The words
of a poem are not merely the signs of concepts: they are also rich
in affective and spiritual associations. The poet uses words not merely to make declarations, statements of fact. That is usually the last
thing that concerns him. He seeks above all to put words together
in such a way that they exercise a mysterious and vital reactivity
among themselves, and so release their secret content of associations to produce in the reader an experience that enriches the
depths of his spirit in a manner quite unique. A good poem induces
an experience that could not be produced by any other combination of words. It is therefore an entity that stands by itself, graced
with an individuality that marks it off from every other work of art.
Like all great works of art, true poems seem to live by a life entirely
their own. What we must seek in a poem is therefore not an accidental reference to something outside itself: we must seek this
inner principle of individuality and of life which is its soul, or
"form." What the poem actually "means" can only be summed up
in the whole content of poetic experience which it is capable of
producing in the reader. This total poetic experience is what the
poet is trying to communicate to the rest of the world.

It is supremely important for those who read the Psalms and
chant them in the public prayer of the Church to grasp, if they can,
the poetic content of these great songs. The poetic gift is not one
that has been bestowed on all men with equal lavishness and that
gift is unfortunately necessary not only for the writers of poems but
also, to some extent, for those who read them. This does not mean
that the recitation of the Divine Office is an aesthetic recreation
whose full possibilities can only be realized by initiates endowed
with refined taste and embellished by a certain artistic cultivation.
But it does mean that the type of reader whose poetic appetites are

53

fully satisfied by the Burma Shave rhymes along our American highways may find it rather hard to get anything out of the Psalms. I believe, however, that the reason why so many fail to understand the Psalms—beyond the fact that they are never quite at home even with Church Latin—is that latent poetic faculties have never been awakened in their spirits by someone capable of pointing out to them that the Psalms really are poems.

Since, then, they are poems, the function of the Psalms is to make us share in the poetic experience of the men who wrote them. No matter how carefully and how scientifically we may interpret the words of the Psalms, and study their historical background, if these investigations do not help us to enter into the poetic experience which the Psalms convey, they are of limited value in showing us what God has revealed in the Psalms, for the revealed content of the Psalter is *poetic*. Let it therefore be clear, that since the inspired writer is an instrument of the Holy Spirit, who, according to the Catholic Faith, is the true Author of the Psalms, what is revealed in the Psalter is revealed in the *poetry* of the Psalter and is only fully apprehended in a poetic experience that is analogous to the experience of the inspired writer. However, when I speak of the poetry of the Psalter and the content conveyed by its poetic form, I do not mean to imply that it is necessary for everyone to read or recite the Psalms in their original Hebrew, in which alone they possess their authentic and integral artistic form. I imagine that every contemplative would, at some time or other, wish that he could chant the Psalms in the same language in which they were chanted by Jesus on this earth, and in which He quoted them when He was dying on the Cross! This is a longing that very few of us will ever be able to satisfy. But it is accidental.

Actually, the simplicity and universality of the Psalms as poetry makes them accessible to every mind, in every age and in any tongue and I believe that one's poetic sense must be unusually deadened if one has never at any time understood the Psalms without being in some way moved by their deep and universal religious quality.

The Psalms are more than poems: they are *religious* poems. This

II

POETRY SYMBOLISM

AND TYPOLOGY

means that the experience which they convey, and which the reader must try to share, is not only a poetic but a religious experience. Religious poetry—as distinct from merely devotional verse—is poetry that springs from a true religious experience. I do not necessarily mean a mystical experience. Devotional poetry is verse which manipulates religious themes and which does so, perhaps, even on a truly poetic level. But the experiential content of the poem is at best poetic only. Sometimes it is not even that. Much of what passes for "religious" verse is simply the rearrangement of well known devotional formulas, without any personal poetic assimilation at all. It is a game, in which souls, no doubt sincere in their piety, play poetic checkers with a certain number of familiar devotional clichés. This activity is prompted by a fundamentally religious intention, if the poem be written for the glory of God or for the salvation of souls. But such poems rarely "save" any souls. They flatter those who are comfortably "saved" but irritate the ones who really need salvation. A truly religious poem is not born merely of a religious purpose. Neither poetry nor contemplation is built out of good

intentions. Indeed, a poem that springs from no deeper spiritual need than a devout intention will necessarily appear to be at the same time forced and tame. Art that is simply "willed" is not art, and it tends to have the same disquieting effect upon the reader as forced piety and religious strain in those who are trying hard to be contemplatives, as if infused contemplation were the result of human effort rather than a gift of God. It seems to me that such poetry were better not written. It tends to confirm unbelievers in their suspicion that religion deadens instead of nurtures all that is vital in the spirit of man. The Psalms, on the other hand, are at the same time the simplest and the greatest of all religious poems.

No one will question the truly religious content of the Psalms. They are the songs of men—and David was the greatest of them— for whom God was more than an abstract idea, more than a frozen watchmaker sitting in his tower while his universe goes ticking away into space without him. Nor is the God of the Psalms simply an absolute, immanent Being spinning forth from some deep metaphysical womb an endless pageantry of phenomena. The Psalms are not incantations to lull us to sleep in such a one.

The human symbolism of the Psalter, primitive and simple as it is, should not deceive us into thinking that David had an "anthropomorphic" God. Such a mistake could only be made by materialists who had lost all sense of poetic form and who, moreover, had forgotten the violent insistence of the great Jewish prophets on the transcendence, the infinite spirituality of Jaweh, Who was so far above all things imaginable that He did not even have an utterable name. The God of the Psalter is "above all gods," that is to say, above anything that could possibly be represented and adored in an image. To one who can penetrate the poetic content of the Psalter, it is clear that David's concept of God was utterly pure. And yet this God, Who is "above all the heavens" is "near to those who call upon Him." He Who is above all things is also in all things, and He is capable of manifesting Himself through them all. [27]

The men who wrote the Psalms were carried away in an ecstasy of joy when they saw God in the cosmic symbolism of His created universe.

> *The heavens declare the glory of God, and the firmament proclaims the work of his hands.*
> *Day unto day heralds the message, and night unto night makes it known.*
> *There is no speech nor words, whose voice is not heard :*
> *Their sound goes forth unto all the earth, and their strains unto the farthest bounds of the world.*
> *There he has set his tabernacle for the sun, which like to the bridegroom coming out from the bridal chamber, he exults like a giant to run his course.*
> *His going forth is from one end of the heavens, and his circuit ends at the other . . .* [28]
> *Praise ye the Lord from the heavens, praise ye him in the high places.*
> *Praise ye him, all his angels, praise ye him, all his hosts.*
> *Praise ye him, O sun and moon, praise him, all ye shining stars.*
> *Praise him, ye heavens of heavens, and ye waters that are above the heavens :*
> *Let them praise the name of the Lord, for he commanded and they were created,*
> *And he established them for ever and ever : he gave a decree, which shall*

II

POETRY SYMBOLISM

AND TYPOLOGY

not pass away.
Praise the Lord from the earth, ye sea-monsters and all ye depths of the sea.
Fire and hail, snow and mist, stormy wind, that fulfil his word,
Mountains and all hills, fruitful trees and all cedars,
Beasts and all cattle, serpents and feathered fowls,
Kings of the earth and all people, princes and all judges of the earth,
Young men and even maidens, old men together with children :
Let them praise the name of the Lord, for his name alone is exalted; [29]

Although we tend to look upon the Old Testament as a chron-
icle of fear in which men were far from their God, we forget how
many of the patriarchs and prophets seem to have walked with God
with some of the intimate simplicity of Adam in Eden. This is especially evident in the first days of the Patriarchs, of which the
Welsh metaphysical poet Henry Vaughan, speaks when he says:

My God, when I walke in those groves,
And leaves thy spirit doth still fan,
I see in each shade that there growes
An Angell talking with a man
Under a juniper some house,
Or the coole mirtles canopie,
Others beneath an oakes greene boughs,
Or at some fountaines bubling Eye;
Here Jacob dreames, and wrestles; there
Elias by a Raven is fed,
Another time by th' Angell, where
He brings him water with his bread;
In Abr'hams Tent the winged guests
(O how familiar then was heaven!)
Eate, drinke, discourse, sit downe, and rest
Untill the Coole, and shady even;"

Poetry, Symbolism & Typology

As age succeeded age the memory of this primitive revelation of God
seems to have withered away, but its leaf is still green in the Psalter.
David is drunk with the love of God and filled with the primitive

sense that man is the *Leitourgos* or the high priest of all creation, born with the function of uttering in "Liturgy" the whole testimony of praise which mute creation cannot of itself offer to its God.

The function of cosmic symbols in the Psalter is an important one. The revelation of God to man through nature is not the exclusive property of any one religion. It is shared by the whole human race and forms the foundation for all natural religions.[30] At the same time the vision of God in nature is a natural preamble to supernatural faith, which depends upon distinct and supernatural revelation. Hence even those modern readers who may be repelled by the "historical" Psalms, will nevertheless be attracted by those in which the keynote is struck by cosmic symbolism, and by the vision of God in nature.

However, the cosmic symbolism in the Old Testament is something much more than an element which Judaeo-Christian revelation shares with the cults of the Gentiles. The Old Testament writers, and particularly the author of the creation narrative that opens the *Book of Genesis,* were not only dealing with symbolic themes which had made their appearance in other religions of the Near East: they were consciously attempting to purify and elevate the cosmic symbols which were the common heritage of all mankind and restore to them a dignity of which they had been robbed by being degraded from the level of theistic symbols to that of polytheistic myths.

This question is so important that I hope I may be permitted a brief digression in order to touch upon it.[31]

Everyone knows with what enthusiasm the rationalists of the late nineteenth century berated the Judaeo-Christian revelation for being fabricated out of borrowed materials, because the religious themes and symbols of the Old Testament were similar to those of many other Eastern religions, and because the New Testament made use of language and concepts which bore a great resemblance to the formulas of Platonic philosophy, the ritual language of the mystery cults and the mythological structure of other Oriental beliefs. Even today the world is full of honest persons who suppose that this parallelism somehow weakens the Christian claim to an exclusive divine revelation. The writers of the Old and New Testament were

II

POETRY SYMBOLISM

AND TYPOLOGY

simple men, but St John the Evangelist was certainly not so simple as to imagine that the Greek word *logos,* which he may well have borrowed from the Platonists, was a personal discovery of his own. The fact that the Biblical writers were inspired did not deliver them from the common necessity which compels writers to clothe their ideas in words taken from the current vocabulary of their culture and of their time. When God inspired the author of *Genesis* with the true account of the creation of the world, the writer might, by some miracle, have set the whole thing down in the vocabulary of a twentieth century textbook of paleontology. But that would have made *Genesis* quite inaccessible to anyone except a twentieth century student of paleontology. So instead, the Creation narrative was set down in the form of a poem which made free use of the cosmic symbolism which was common to all primitive mankind.

Light and darkness, sun and moon, stars and planets, trees, beasts, whales, fishes and birds of the air, all these things in the world around us and the whole natural economy in which they have Poetry, Symbolism & Typology their place have impressed themselves upon the spirit of man in such a way that they naturally tend to mean to him much more than they mean in themselves. That is why, for example, they enter so mysteriously into the substance of our poetry, of our visions and of our dreams. That too is why an age, like the one we live in, in which cosmic symbolism has been almost forgotten and submerged under a tidal wave of trademarks, political party buttons, advertising and propaganda slogans and all the rest—is necessarily an age of mass psychosis. A world in which the poet can find practically no material in the common substance of every day life, and in which he is driven crazy in his search for the vital symbols that have been buried alive under a mountain of cultural garbage, can only end up, like ours, in self-destruction. And that is why some of the best poets of our time are running wild among the tombs in the moonlit cemeteries of surrealism. Faithful to the instincts of the true poet, they are unable to seek their symbols anywhere save in the depths of the spirit where these symbols are found. These depths have become a ruin and a slum. But poetry must, and does, make good use of whatever it finds there: starvation, madness, frustration and death.

Now the writers of the Bible were aware that they shared with other religions, the cosmic symbols in which God has revealed Himself to all men. But they were also aware that pagan and idolatrous religions had corrupted this symbolism and perverted its original purity[32]. The Gentiles had "detained the truth of God in injustice"[33] and "changed the truth of God into a lie."[34]

Creation had been given to man as a clean window through which the light of God could shine into men's souls. Sun and moon, night and day, rain, the sea, the crops, the flowering tree, all these things were transparent. They spoke to man not of themselves only but of Him who made them. Nature was symbolic. But the progressive degradation of man after the fall led the Gentiles further and further from this truth. Nature became opaque. The nations were no longer able to penetrate the meaning of the world they lived in. Instead of seeing the sun a witness to the power of God, they thought the sun was god. The whole universe became an enclosed system of myths. The meaning and the worth of creatures invested them with an illusory divinity.

II

POETRY SYMBOLISM

AND TYPOLOGY

Men still sensed that there was something to be venerated in the reality, in the peculiarity of living and growing things but they no longer knew what that reality was. They became incapable of seeing that the goodness of the creature is only a vestige of God. Darkness settled upon the translucent universe. Men became afraid. Beings had a meaning which men could no longer understand. They became afraid of trees, of the sun, of the sea. These things had to be approached with superstitious rites. It began to seem that the mystery of their meaning, which had become hidden, was now a power that had to be placated and, if possible, controlled by magic incantations.

Thus the beautiful living things which were all about us on this earth and which were the windows of heaven to every man, became infected with original sin. The world fell with man, and longs, with man, for regeneration. The symbolic universe, which had now become a labyrinth of myths and magic rites, the dwelling place of a million hostile spirits, ceased altogether to speak to most men of

God and told them only of themselves. The *symbols* which would have raised man above himself to God now became *myths* and as such they were simply projections of man's own biological drives. His deepest appetites, now full of shame, became his darkest fears.

The corruption of cosmic symbolism can be understood by a simple comparison. It was like what happens to a window when a room ceases to receive light from the outside. As long as it is daylight, we see through our windowpane. When night comes, we can still see through it, if there is no light inside our room. When our lights go on, then we only see ourselves and our own room reflected in the pane. Adam in Eden could see through creation as through a window. God shone through the windowpane as bright as the light of the sun. Abraham and the patriarchs and David and the holy men of Israel—the chosen race that preserved intact the testimony of God—could still see through the window as one looks out by night from a darkened room and sees the moon and stars. But the Gentiles had begun to forget the sky, and to light lamps of their own, and presently it seemed to them that the reflection of their own room in the window was the "world beyond." They began to worship what they themselves were doing. And what they were doing was too often an abomination. Nevertheless, something of the original purity of natural revelation remained in the great religions of the East. It is found in the *Upanishads* in the *Baghavad Gita*. But the pessimism of Buddha was a reaction against the degeneration of nature by polytheism. Henceforth for the mysticisms of the East, nature would no longer be symbol but illusion. Buddha knew too well that the reflections in the window were only projections of our own existence and our own desires, but did not know that this was a window, and that there could be sunlight outside the glass.

So much, then, for cosmic symbols. In the Psalms we find them clean and bright again, where David sings:

O Lord, our Lord, how glorious is thy name in all the earth, thou who hast exalted thy majesty above the heavens . . .
When I gaze at the heavens, the work of thy fingers, the moon and stars, which thou hast made:

What is man, that thou are mindful of him? or the son of man,
*   that thou hast care of him?*
And thou hast made him a little lower than the angels,
*   thou hast crowned him with glory and honor;*
Thou hast given him dominion over the works of thy hands;
*   thou hast put all things under his feet:*
Sheep and oxen, all of them, and the beasts of the field, too,
The birds of the heaven and the fishes of the sea:
*   and whatever traverses the paths of the seas.*
O Lord, our Lord, how wonderful is thy name in all the earth! [35]

But it is not the cosmic symbolism that is the most important symbolism in the Bible. There is another. This is the symbolism we have already referred to as *typology*. The typological symbolism of the Bible is not common to other religions: its content is peculiar to the Judaeo-Christian revelation. It is the vehicle of the special message, the "Gospel" which is the very essence of Christian revelation. And it is typology above all that makes the Psalms a body of religious poems which are, by their own right, altogether unique.

I have already brought up the subject of the typical sense of the Psalter. I have discussed the significance of type and antitype, and suggested briefly that the important antitypes in Scripture all have something to do with the Incarnation of the Word of God, and with man's Redemption by the Sacrifice of Christ on Calvary, for this is the central Mystery of the Christian faith. It is now time to add a few remarks on the importance of typology in the Psalms.

Pope Pius XII said, we remember, that "By assuming human nature, the Divine Word introduced into this exile a hymn which is sung in heaven for all eternity." The context of this important declaration suggested to us that if the Psalter and the Liturgy can become for us means to contemplation, it is simply because they are capable of uniting us with Christ in this "hymn which is sung in heaven." That is as much as to say that if the Psalter is to lead us to contemplation we must know how to find Christ in the Psalms. Apart from a few clear messianic prophecies it is typology that reveals Christ to us, even in some of the most unexpected lines of the Psalms.

II

POETRY SYMBOLISM

AND TYPOLOGY

Scriptural typology is a special kind of symbolism. It is something far purer and more efficacious than allegory. I would even add that in the Psalms allegory is altogether negligible. There is almost nothing in the Psalter that reminds us of the tissue of allegorical complexities which goes to make up a poem like Spenser's *Faerie Queene*. It seems to me that the personification of moral abstractions is foreign to the spirit of true contemplation.

The relation of types and antitypes in Scripture is a special manifestation of God: it is the testimony of His continuous providential intervention in human history. Unlike the universal cosmic symbols, which repeat themselves over and over with the seasons, historical and typical symbols are altogether singular. Cosmic symbols reflect the action of God like the light of the sun on the vast sea of creation. Typological symbols are meteors which divide the dark sky of history with a sudden, searing light, appearing and vanishing with a liberty that knows no law of man. Cosmic symbolism is like clouds and rain: but typology is like a storm of lightning wounding the earth unpredictably with fire from heaven.

Consider for a moment the typology of the Deluge. In the Deluge, God purifies the world, destroying sin. The Deluge is simply a type of the one great redemptive act in which God destroyed sin: Christ's passion and death. But the symbolism of the Deluge goes further: it also manifests to us the activity of God destroying sin in the souls of individuals by the sacraments, for instance Baptism and Penance, in which the merits of Christ's Passion are applied to our souls. This also corresponds to another Old Testament type: the crossing of the Red Sea by the people of Israel. Finally, all these symbols are tied together in one, final, climax of significance. All Scriptural types point to the last end, the crowning of Christ's work, the establishment of His Kingdom, His final and manifest triumph in His mystical body: the Last Judgment. There again, the same creative action by which God manifested Himself in the Deluge will once more strike the world of sin. But this time it will have the nature of a final "accounting" in the sense that then all men will come forth to give testimony to their personal response to God's action in the world. Those who have believed, and who have freely accepted the

63

light and the salvation offered to them from heaven, will pass, like the Israelites, through the Red Sea; they will be rescued in Christ as Noah's sons were saved in the Ark; they will have lived out the meaning of their Baptism because they will have died and risen with Christ. Those who were not with Christ—and all who are not with him are against Him—will manifest what they too have chosen. It will be by their own choice that they will drown in the Deluge, and perish with the chariots of Egypt in the closing waters of that last sea.

Not only do many of the Psalms literally foretell the suffering and glory of Christ, but David is a "type" of Christ. The Psalter as a whole is "typical" of the New Testament as a whole and often the particular sentiments of the Psalmist are, at least in a broad sense, "typical" of the sentiments in the Heart of the Divine Redeemer. Even the sins of David belong to Christ, in the sense that "God hath laid upon Him the iniquity of us all." [36]

II

POETRY SYMBOLISM

AND TYPOLOGY

SACRAMENTA SCRIPTURARUM

III

1:

Words as Signs and "Sacraments"

ST AUGUSTINE DOES NOT HESITATE TO APPLY
to the Scriptures the analogical term "sacraments." Nor should
we be surprised at his use of the expression *sacramenta scripturarum*
when we remember, for instance, the external reverence with
which the Church emphasizes the dignity of the Gospel in a Solemn
Mass. It is well known that the Church's reverence for the Scriptures
resembles to some extent the honor she pays to the Blessed Sacrament Itself.

The Scriptures are one of the Church's greatest sacramentals,
for the "Word of God is living and effectual and more piercing
than any two-edged sword and reaching unto the division of the
soul and the spirit, of the joints also and the marrow, and is a dis-
cerner also of the thoughts and intents of the heart."[37]

All the revealed words of God are partial manifestations of the
Word, Who is the splendor of God's Truth. All the revealed words
of God are, as it were, species under which is hidden the one
Word, Who is the way, the truth and the life. That is why Jesus,
the word made flesh, could calmly say: "Search the Scriptures...
the same are they that give testimony of me." He was speaking to
the Doctors of the Law, who were right in hoping to find in the
Scriptures "life everlasting" : but they were wrong in expecting
that the life, promised by the Scriptures and contained in them,
would be anything or anyone but Jesus. Therefore our Lord added
"and you will not come to me that you may have life."[38] St Paul
showed clearly that Christ was the "end of the Law," that is the
fulfilment of the whole Old Testament. He is the life contained in
the revealed word and communicated by it. "The word is nigh
thee, even in thy mouth and in thy heart. This is the word of faith,
which we preach, for if thou confess with thy mouth the Lord Jesus
and believe in thy heart that God hath raised Him from the dead,
thou shalt be saved."[39]

Of whom can it more truly be said that the "word is nigh them,
even their mouth and in their heart," than those who daily recite
or chant the Divine Office? If that word is to become for them living and effectual, if it is to penetrate the depths of their interior
life and make them contemplatives, they must discover in it the

Christ Who is the light of the world. He who is the center of the Old Testament and of the New is, above all, the life of the Psalter. When we recite the Psalms we must learn to recognize in them the suffering and triumphant Messias, confessing Him with our mouth and believing in our heart that God has raised Him from the dead. Then we reap the abundant fruits of His Redemption. The salvific life that flows from His Cross will swell in our heart until it bursts our veins and we will cry out with Philip: " We have found Him of whom Moses and the prophets did write, Jesus the son of Joseph of Nazareth." [40]

III

SACRAMENTA

SCRIPTURARUM

2:

Transformation in Discovery

JUST AS IN THE PATRISTIC AGE THE FAITHFUL
used to bring their gifts to the altar at Mass, and matter for the
Sacrifice was set apart from among the offerings of bread and wine,
so we who recite the Psalms for the whole Church bring to this
"action" our own matter for sacrifice. I use the word action advisedly, because all liturgical prayer is an action, and it is all a more
or less close participation in the one central Redemptive Act of Sacrifice which is the heart of our Liturgy as it is of our religion and
of all human history: the death and resurrection of Jesus Christ.
We ought to consider the Psalms of the Office as an extension of
the Mass, and find in them the movement of the same action which is
the Sacrifice of the Mass. And so, here too, there is an "offertory"
and we bring matter for sacrifice. We bring our sorrows, our problems, our difficulties, and immerse them in Psalms. We bring our
personal struggles and interior conflicts and offer them up to God
the Father, not in our own words but in those of the Psalms. We
identify ourselves with the one who suffers, who struggles, who
labors—and who triumphs—in the Psalter.

At first, this may not be very illuminating. It may not give us
much comfort. Nevertheless we must persevere in faith and in
desire. We must go on plunging our leprosy, like Naaman, in this
Jordan, this stream of Psalmody. Like Naaman we may be strangers,
and our hearts may hark back to all the rivers of Damascus, and we
may feel very little kinship with this man in the Psalms whose joys
and sorrows are dressed in language so unlike our own. And yet the
very unfamiliarity of Scriptural language, says St Augustine, has its
purpose.[41] The language of revelation is mysterious not in order
that its meaning may be concealed from us, but in order that we
may be moved to seek it with a more fervent love. For God only
reveals His secrets to those who love Him, and who seek to know
Him in order to love Him better.

When we bring our sorrows to the Psalter we find all our spiritual problems mirrored in the inspired words of the Psalmist.
But we do not necessarily find these problems analyzed and solved.
Few of the Psalms offer us abstract principles capable of serving as
a ready and sensible palliative for interior suffering. On the con-

trary, what we generally find is a suffering just as concrete as our own, and more profound. We encounter this suffering at one of its most intense and articulate moments. How many of the Psalms are simply cries of desperate anguish: "Save me, O God, for the waters have come up to my neck. I am plunged into the mire of the deep and there is nowhere to set my foot; I am come into deep waters and the waves overwhelm me. I am wearied with crying; my throat has become hoarse; my eyes have failed, while I await my God."[42]

What were the dispositions of the saints and the Fathers, in chanting such a Psalm? They did not simply "consider" the Psalm as they passed over it, drawing from it some pious reflection, or twirling one of its verses between their fingers as a spiritual nosegay. They entered into the "action" of the Psalm. They allowed themselves to be absorbed in the spiritual agony of the Psalmist and of the One he represented. They allowed their sorrows to be swallowed up in the sorrows of this mysterious Personage and then they found themselves swept away, on the strong tide of his hope, into the very depths of God. "But unto thee, O Lord, is my prayer, in the time of mercy, O God; Hear me, O God, in thy great goodness, according to thy faithful help." [43] So, in the end, all sorrow turns to triumph and to praise: "I will praise the name of God with song, and I will glorify Him with thanksgiving . . . For God will save Sion and build up the cities of Juda and they shall dwell therein and possess it. And the seed of his servants shall inherit it and they that love His name shall abide therein."[44]

III

SACRAMENTA
SCRIPTURARUM

We too, when we chant these verses as the old saints must have chanted them, experience the truth which the Fathers reveal to us in their writings. We find out that when we bring our own sorrows and desires and hopes and fears to God and plunge them all into the sorrows and hopes of the mysterious One who sings this Psalm, a kind of transubstantiation is effected. We have put all that we have—or rather all our poverty, all that we have not—into the hands of Christ. He who is Everything and has everything pronounces over our gift words of His own. Consecrated by contact with the poverty He assumed to deliver us, we find that in His poverty our poverty becomes infinite riches: in His sufferings our defeats are transubstantiated into victory, and His death becomes our everlasting life.

What has happened? We have been transformed. The process is more than a tragic *catharsis*. This is more than the psychological impact of a work of art, in which our emotions, clenched in a dramatic crisis, have been sprung, have been released, and have achieved a vital fulfilment by a successful poetic solution of the problem in which we have allowed ourselves to become emotionally involved. There is something much deeper. It is a spiritual solution. It is a kind of death and a sea-change, operated as it were at the bottom of a spiritual ocean, because it can just as well happen to us when the Psalm, having become insipid to us by continual repetition, has ceased to have any immediate artistic appeal. And I may add that it might even happen to someone who has never quite been attuned to the full poetic quality of the Psalms.

This transformation is operated in us by the power of the Holy Spirit Who lives and acts in the word He has inspired. He, if you like, is the poet. But He also is the poetry. Or rather Christ, Whose Spirit He is, is the poetry of the Psalms. But the Holy Spirit, besides being the artist, is also the spectator. He is at the same time the poet, the poetry and the reader of the poetry; the music and the musician, the singer and the hearer. The peculiar mystical impact with which certain verses of Psalms suddenly produce this silent depth-charge in the heart of the contemplative is only to be accounted for by the fact that we, in the Spirit, recognize the Spirit singing in ourselves.

We are transformed in the midst of a discovery. What discovery? God's discovery of Himself in His own Psalm. Only God is really capable of appreciating the things contained in the verses God has written. The word of God is full of the Word of God. Christ is conceived in human language through the Holy Ghost, as He was conceived in human flesh, of the Holy Ghost. The Christ Who is born to us of Scripture is just as hard to recognize as the Christ Who is born to us of Mary. In fact, He cannot be recognized unless His Spirit recognize Him in us, illuminating our minds with his secret presence. "A man cannot receive anything unless it be given him from heaven."[45] Such was the testimony of John the Precursor

75

who told all Israel that he himself would never have recognized the Messias unless he had seen the Spirit descending upon Him from heaven.[46] Only the Spirit of God can point out Christ to us. But the instant in which he does so opens to us something of the depths of that infinite and eternal flash of recognition in which God sees and loves Himself. God's discovery of Himself has been going on for ever. So great a thing is this discovery of God by God that its moments are the processions of Divine Persons. The Father, the Beholder, is a Person. His Vision is the generation of a Person. Love springs from this Vision, proceeds and is another Person, and these Three are one Discovery of their own one infinite Actuality. Jahweh, *Ego sum, I am.*

"To as many as received Him," writes St John the Evangelist of the Word made flesh, "He gave the power to become the sons of God."[47]

III

SACRAMENTA

SCRIPTURARUM

The acceptance of this grace of recognition, in which the Spirit signifies to us, by the touch of a secret experience, that Christ speaks, sings, suffers, triumphs in a Psalm, is a new awakening to our own divine sonship. We lift up our heads in the valley of the shadow and we draw breath, and light momentarily trembles in our eyes that have been too long filled with the waters of death. Then our spirit cracks the walls of its tomb with something of the power Christ shed into our souls on the morning of His Resurrection.

Fear has been turned into fortitude. Anguish has become joy without somehow ceasing to be anguish and we triumph over suffering not by escaping it but by completely accepting it. This is the only triumph, because there is no victory in evasion.

More than that, we ourselves have become Someone else. We remain ourselves, fully ourselves. Yet we are aware of a new principle of activity. We are fulfilled by an Identity that does not annihilate our own, which is ours, and yet is "received." It is a Person eternally other than ourselves who identifies Himself perfectly with ourselves. This Identity is Christ, God. We discover something of the theological reality that human nature has been, by Him, not absorbed, but *assumed.* He took to Himself a concrete individual nature: but that nature was our nature, and by virtue of this assumption, it was I who died with Him on the Cross, I who rose with Him to sit at the right hand of the Father in Heaven because it is He who now still suffers and dies in me on this earth of bitter battle and sin. *Convivificavit nos in Christo* "He has given us all life together in Christ" *Consedere nos fecit in caelestibus in Christo Jesu:* "He has enthroned us together in heaven with Christ Jesus," says St Paul.[48] And the Church asks in her prayer for Ascension Day that we may always live thus with Christ, Who is our Life, in Heaven.[49]

3:

"*Visible Mysteries*"

SINCE WE HAVE JUST SPOKEN OF THE MASS OF Ascension Day, let us take up another idea that is emphasized in that Mass. The Postcommunion prayer is one of the many dogmatic statements of the spiritual power that is exercised upon souls, by the Holy Ghost, through the Mysteries and Sacraments of the Faith, to transform men into Christ. The prayer runs: "Grant us, we beseech Thee, O almighty and merciful Lord, that what we have received as our nourishment in visible Mysteries we may enjoy in its invisible effect." [50]

What is meant by the term "visible Mysteries"? It is evident from this particular context that it is an expression which the liturgical language of the Church uses when it speaks of Holy Communion. And of course it refers not to Communion in the abstract, but to Communion as the vital act of participation in the Sacrifice of the Mass by receiving the Body of Christ. The word "Mysteries," in the liturgical language of the Church, means the Mass, in all its essentials and all its integral parts and all its accidents. The "Sacred Mysteries" are the Mass and all that surrounds the Mass. The ceremonies and functions of the Divine Office are not usually referred to as "Mysteries." However, they bear a close relation to the Mass which is the center of the whole Liturgy. What is more, there is a whole gamut of meanings in which the word "Mysteries" transcends its merely liturgical reference. And the Mystery of Faith in these higher and broader senses is also contained in Scripture and is accessible above all in the Gospels and the Psalms.

In the first place, God Himself, the Holy Trinity, is the infinite Mystery and of Him all other "Mysteries" are a revelation. He manifests Himself to us in the "Mysteries" with which the Scriptures are filled. But above all He has spoken to us directly in His Son, *locutus est nobis in Filio*. [51]

It is also customary to speak of the "Mysteries of Christ." These "Mysteries" are groups of significant actions in the Life of Jesus— the Mystery of the Nativity, of the Hidden Life, the Baptism, the Passion, and so on—considered as God's revelations of Himself to us in Christ. For Christ, the Man, is the Word of God and all His actions and virtues as man give the most perfect possible human expression

III

SACRAMENTA

SCRIPTURARUM

to the Life He leads as Word *in sinu Patris,* in the depths of the God-head. His Sacrifice of Himself on the Cross for us, an unfathomable Mystery of disinterested Love, is a most perfect concrete expression of that Charity which is the very Nature of God : for God is Love.

These "Mysteries" of Christ are not merely called "Mysteries" because they are too deep for us to understand and are therefore proposed to us to be contemplated with silent and adoring faith. They are not just something you think about and look at. The term *mysterium* in St Paul has a dynamic sense. It is the fulfilment of a divine plan, springing forth from the eternal wisdom of God, producing its effect in time and, by virtue of this effect, elevating men from the level of time to that of eternity, from the human level to the divine.

Now it is by the redemptive sufferings and death of Christ that men are elevated above a natural order which Adam's sin and all the sins that grew from it had turned into an endless cycle of frustrations. Therefore the true Mystery of Christ, the one central Mystery of Faith to which everything else points, is not the Incarnation alone, or the Public Life of Christ, but His Passion, Death, and Resurrection from the dead.

Nor do we enter into that Mystery most fully by thinking about it or by producing in our hearts the affections which such a meditation might inspire. It is necessary that the full power of this theandric action of Christ which is the summit of all Mysteries, should enter into our lives and be prolonged in them. How is this to be done? Christ has bequeathed this theandric action of His to His Church. He has given her the Mass, which perpetuates and daily renews, not in symbol only but in literal fact, the Sacrifice of Calvary. Hence this Mystery of Mysteries is not merely something that once happened, the memory of which is preserved for our study and admiration. The central Mystery of the Faith is living and efficacious and is in the possession of Christ's Mystical Body, the Church. But does the Church merely possess this Sacrifice as a rite which she exercises, as it were, exteriorly, without entering into it herself? Then the Blessed Eucharist would merely be a drama, not a Sacrament.

The Mystery of Faith would then be no more of a mystery than a medieval mystery play.

In order to receive the effects of the Sacrifice of Christ, the Church has to offer herself completely to God, with Christ. The Body must be united in all things with its Head, or it is not a living body and does not live the life of the Head. The Church, say some of the Fathers, was born when blood and water (signifying the Sacraments) flowed from the pierced side of Christ on Calvary. If this be so, then the very nature and identity of the Church are inseparable from the notion of Christ's Sacrifice. She exists by virtue of that Sacrifice, she goes on existing in order to continue that Sacrifice and her final exaltation will be the consummation of that Sacrifice. The Church is nothing else but the Mystical Body of those who have been baptized in Christ's death, [52] and who, by that fact, have risen to a new life in God with Him Who is both God and Man. This participation in the theandric action by which Christ redeemed the world is nothing merely passive. The Church must take a living and active part in the Mystery of Christ. The Sacrifice of the Mass is, therefore, just as much hers as it is His. The Church is a Body of living members and what we say, abstractly, of her, must be verified concretely in them. We, who live in Christ, possess and offer the Sacrifice which is one great Mystery. In this Mystery God supernaturally manifests Himself in the world, enters temporally into the stream of human history in order to sanctify part of that stream for Himself and bring it into the ocean of eternity.

The priest at the altar more than represents Christ. When the Sacred Species are consecrated, it is Christ Who speaks through the priest in His own Name and in the first Person: "This is MY body." That same priest turns from the altar to the people and says: "Pray brethren that my sacrifice and yours may be acceptable to God the Father almighty." The Sacrifice, the Mystery, belongs to all of us who love God because in it we are all offered to the Father in and with Christ, all enter into His Passion and rise with Him from the dead. The union of each one of us with Christ is not merely moral and symbolic, it is physical and real because Jesus and His Church are physically united in the Sacrifice offered by the priest.

However, this union has a double aspect. It is true that the Sacraments produce grace *ex opere operato*. This physical union is effected

3. *"Visible Mysteries"*

81

by the mere fact that the Sacraments are conferred upon a subject that is properly disposed. But as soon as we speak of the dispositions of the one receiving the Sacrament we are in the moral or, if you prefer, the ascetic order. In actual practice, we must enter into the mysteries of Christ not only sacramentally but also ascetically because the sacramental order is meant to be fulfilled by our application of the graces of the Sacraments to our own lives. This means that we share in Christ's Passion and Resurrection not merely in a hidden and mystical sense, but also by active imitation of His virtues. To enter into His Mysteries means to die, as He died, to the desires of the flesh and to rise to a new life in the Spirit. This cannot be done without suffering and self-sacrifice. Jesus Himself made it clear that the asceticism He demanded of His disciples was an essential condition of that union with Him in the Mysteries in which He overcame death. "He who does not take up his cross and follow me, is not worthy of me. He that would save his life will lose it, and he that would lose his life for my sake shall find it." [53]

Just as Jesus patiently suffered injustice, calumny, abuse and physical torture, so too we must make an effort to accept the hardships and pains and trials and misfortunes of life, and even to embrace voluntary privations and sacrifices, with something of His gentleness, humility and love. The Mass is our Sacrifice only if we offer ourselves in it, with Christ, to God. But our offering is meaningless if it does not represent some willingness to verify our offering in self-sacrifice.

Therefore, in actual fact, it is by this *ascetic prolongation* of the sacramental life of the Church that Christ wills to manifest and realize in each one of us the Mystery of Faith, which is the greatest revelation of the love of God. The whole Christian ascesis is built up like a pyramid. It is an ascending scale of the reconciliation of opposites. Strength must combine with gentleness, humility with courage, the prudence of the serpent with the simplicity of the dove. But at the top of the pyramid is that charity which is the summary of all the virtues and the life and form of them all because in it is perfected our union with the God Who is Love. By this love for God and for one another we give evidence that we have entered into the Mystery of Christ's Sacrifice. Charity is not only the fulfilment of the Law but the fulfilment of the "Mysteries." Charity must be the fruit of all devotion, all asceticism, and above all of the Liturgy, because without charity the Liturgy is only a tinkling cymbal.

That is why the Mass is called the Sacrament of Love. The Eucharist is the *sacramentum unitatis*. Christ, in His high priestly prayer at the Last Supper (a prayer which forms the model and the basis of the Canon of the Mass) prayed to the Father to make all souls one in His Mystery. "I in them and Thou in me, that they may be consummated in one and that the world may know that Thou hast sent me, and hast loved them as thou hast loved me." [54]

Clearly, this unity of the faithful in charity is the full expression of the Mystery of Christ on earth. In this charity the light of the Mass is poured out upon the world, for Jesus makes it evident that it is above all by our union with one another in Him that the Father's love for us is made known to men. It is therefore insufficient to consider the Mass merely as legal Sacrifice for the expiation of sin: we must see it also, as the early Christians did, as a feast of love, an *agape*. We must look at it through the eyes of the great theologian of the Blessed Eucharist, St Thomas Aquinas, who wrote: "the full spiritual reality *(res sacramenti)* of this Sacrament of the Eucharist is *the unity of the Body of Christ.*" [55]

3. *"Visible Mysteries"*

St Leo the Great teaches, in the strongest terms, the reality of this physical union of the Christian with Christ through the worthy reception of the Sacraments, prolonged and expressed by the ascetic life of charity that culminates in contemplation. "The body of the man who is reborn in Christ *becomes the very flesh of Christ." (Corpus regenerati fit caro Christi.)*[56] In all those who prove the vitality of their union with Christ by works of charity, it is Christ Himself who does their good works in them, says the Saint *(ipsum piorum operum intelligamus auctorem.)* [57]

Christ, he continues, pours out His graces upon the whole Church in such a way that the actions of Christians shine like rays of light emanating from the one sun, who is Christ. That is why the merits of the Saints all give glory to Christ. They are expressions of

83

the power of Christ and bear witness to the sanctity of Christ—the sanctity which He has received from His Father from all eternity, and which He has communicated to them.

The effect of our communion in the Body and Blood of Christ is that we are transformed into what we consume, and that He in Whom we have died and in Whom we have risen from the dead, lives and is manifested in every movement of our body and of our spirit.[58]

III

SACRAMENTA

SCRIPTURARUM

4:

"When Israel came out of Egypt..."

THE PSALTER CANNOT BE APPRECIATED UNTIL
it is seen in the light of the great Mystery of Faith which is centered
in the Mass. There is an extraordinarily intimate connection between the Psalter and the Mass. Not only are the sufferings and death
of the Redeemer literally and typically foretold in the Psalms; not
only are the Psalms often chanted in the celebration of the Mass itself,
as part of the Proper of the saints or of the time, but also the very
Canon of the Mass, the most ancient and most sacred of liturgical
prayers, is an echo of the group of Psalms called the *Hallel,* which
were chanted in the Passover rites of the Jews. This is easy to understand, since the Mass, the Sacrifice of the New Law, is the fulfilment
of the sacrifice of the Paschal Lamb which had been instituted, at
God's command, as a type foreshadowing the Sacrifice of Christ,
Agnus Dei, the Lamb of God. The Psalms of the *Hallel* are concerned
with the "Passover," that is the deliverance of the children of Israel
from Egypt, their passage through the Red Sea, their miraculous
preservation in the wilderness of the Arabian Desert and their en-
trance into the Promised Land.

St Paul saw that the Passover contained, in figure and symbol,
the Mystery of Christ. [59] His *Epistle to the Hebrews* is an argument,
based in great measure upon the Psalter, as well as on the Pentateuch,
that the Sacrifice of Christ is the real Passover by which the true
Israel, the Church, is delivered from bondage to Pharaoh (the
world, the devil, sin), is protected in her journey to the Promised
Land and is finally admitted to the peace of perfect union with God
in heaven.

The Psalms, then, are not merely ancient poems which the
Church fancifully adapts to her own liturgical uses. Everything in
them is charged with vital urgency by virtue of the fact that they
are full of Christ. Either they speak to us directly of the Redeemer
Himself in His sufferings, His kingship, His priesthood: or else they
narrate the trials and progress of the Mystical Christ, the Church,
His people. When Israel went out of Egypt and wandered in the
desert, God became a pilgrim with them in the dark years of their
tribulation. He came down to them on the mountain in cloud and
fire, speaking to them through Moses who was a type of Christ. He

fed them in the desert-with manna, foreshadowing the Holy Eucharist. Water sprang from a rock in the desert at the command of Moses, and never ceased to supply them until they settled in the Land of Promise. "The rock," says St Paul, "was Christ." [60]

The Kings of strange desert tribes have survived in the Psalms; they were the enemies of Israel. Their mysterious names do not mean anything definite to us. These kings emerge from the verses of the Psalms like the weird symbolic enemies that menace us in dreams and fade away. They are the powers of evil that are still fighting the Church today. We know that Sisara is dead with the tent peg in his temple, and Jabin's bones long ago whitened in the ravine of Cisson. Yet Jabin and Sisara still rise up from Hell to plague us, though they cannot prevail. But we know, on the nights when their names pass before us, in the small hours, at the chanting of Matins, that the old battles we are celebrating are more than ever actual. Actual too are the same miracles by which Israel overcame her enemies and entered glorious, through divided Jordan, to occupy the Promised Land.

These battles and these victories go on without ceasing, generation after generation and century by century, because the whole Church is still passing out of Egypt, company by company. The shining tribes of Israel are still crossing the desert in the slow, interminable march that Balaam saw from his mountain when his curse against them choked in his gullet and turned into a song of praise:

Then Balaam, turning his face to the desert saw Israel dwelling in tents, tribe by tribe and the Spirit of God rushed down upon him and he prophesied and said:

> *Thus said Balaam, the son of Beor,*
> *Thus said the man whose eyes were stopped up,*
> *Thus said he who heard the speech of God,*
> *Who saw the vision of the Almighty,*
> *Who fell down and his eyes were opened:*
> *How beautiful are thy tents, O Jacob,*
> *And thy camps, O Israel,*
> *Like the wooded valleys*
> *And like gardens all along the streams of water,*

Like tents which the Lord has planted
Next to the rivers, like cedars . . .
God has brought Israel out of Egypt
Strong as a rhinoceros.
The nations shall devour Israel's enemies
And crush their bones and riddle them with arrows.
Israel lay down and slept like a lion
And like a lioness, that no man dares to waken. [61]

We are the children of Abraham, but only if we do the works of Abraham. His faith does not justify us unless it live and act in us and be our faith. Our ancestors overcame Amalec, leaving us an example, showing us how to fight when we, too, cross the desert in our turn. "Christ suffered for us leaving you an example, that you might follow in His steps." [62]

It is in chanting the Psalms that we too are leaving Egypt. The Liturgy is the Church's greatest weapon against her enemies because it is filled with the might of the Mystery which is its center. The Mystery of Christ is the heart of all history and extends backwards and forwards to embrace all time. It was in Christ that Israel crossed the desert and it is in Christ that we, the tribes of Israel, are going up to Jerusalem. [63] The Mystery of Christ is timeless: but we enter into it by consecrating to Him the little part that is ours of history and of time. It is by the Liturgy and its ascetic fulfilment that we do so.

4. "When Israel came out of Egypt"

This is the secret of the Psalms: they contain in themselves all that matters to a Christian of the history of the world, because in a mysterious and quasi-sacramental manner, by virtue of their intimate connection with the Sacrifice of the Mass, the salvation of the world is all worked out in them. Breviary, Psalter and Missal, charged with the grandeur of the Word of God, contain the mighty secret of Christ's spiritual victory. The secret is placed in the hands of each Christian. It only needs to be discovered and fulfilled in our own lives.

The history of Israel—that is of the people of God, the Church —is also in some measure the history of each individual soul in the Church. As in the natural order each individual man is a microcosm, so in the supernatural order each individual soul is a little church, a miniature heaven and a temple of God. Just as the whole people of God is still crossing the desert to the Promised Land, still passing through the Jordan, still building Jerusalem and raising God's temple on Sion, so each individual soul must normally know something of the same journey, the same hunger and thirst, the same battles and prayers, light and darkness, the same sacrifices and the same struggle to build Jerusalem within itself.

Just as Jesus is entirely present in every consecrated Host and also singly present in them all at once, and just as the soul of a man is entirely present in every cell of his body and is also present in its unity over all his whole body, so Christ lives entirely in each individual Christian and singly in them all. By virtue of His Mysteries, His life becomes the life of each Christian as He is also the life of the whole Church. In each one and in all, He is all. *Omnia in omnibus Christus.*

III

SACRAMENTA

SCRIPTURARUM

Our growth in Christ is growth in charity. Charity is created and strengthened within us by the action of the Holy Spirit—most of all in times of trial and sacrifice, because it is then that we are pressed and compelled, by circumstances, to make heroic choices that confirm our union with Christ, and teach us to know Him as He is. For Christ without the Cross is not our Christ. True, He is now the risen Christ. He knows no suffering. He "dieth now no more." But He has wounds. Even though they be glorious, they are wounds. His Cross is not absent from heaven, but it is there the sign of victory. And it will blaze in the heavens when Christ returns in judgment. The Cross is our only glory, says St Paul. [64] He has sketched out the asceticism of tribulation in a verse of *Romans*. We glory, says he, not only in the hope of the glory of the sons of God (as if we were to enter Heaven without suffering) but we especially glory in tribulation, because tribulation makes us patient; our patience under suffering proves us true Christians; and by this proof we have hope; and this hope cannot be shaken because when we have it, the fulness of love is poured out into our hearts by the Holy Ghost. The Holy Ghost, living and acting in our souls, intimately present to us, is Himself God's gift to us. *Caritas Dei diffusa est in cordibus nostris per Spiritum Sanctum qui datus est nobis.* [65]

The more the Spirit of God pours out into our hearts the love of God, the better we are able to know God. The Mystery of Christ is a dark cloud into which we enter that the Spirit may teach us with His lightning. Says St Paul: "We utter the wisdom of God in Mystery, a Mystery which is hidden, which no one of the princes of his world has known . . . which the eye of man hath not seen, nor hath his ear heard, nor hath the thought of it risen up in his heart, but God has prepared it *for those who love Him.* And God has revealed this wisdom to us in His Spirit, for the Spirit looks into all things, even the depths of God." [66]

The deepest abyss of the love of God, and therefore the perfect knowledge of God, can only be entered through the pierced Heart of the Redeemer. This is the narrow gate that leads us to salvation and to glory. The Holy Spirit opens this gate to us, and we have learned that His key is tribulation.

Yet God is not to be found in suffering as such. Sanctity and love are not born in us by the love of pain for pain's own sake. Suffering is not the cause of holiness but only its occasion. Love, expressed in sacrifice, is what makes us saints. We are made saints not by undergoing pain but by overcoming it. That is why the Cross means joy and not despair, life and not death, fulfilment and not annihilation. All this is the work of the Spirit in our souls, uniting us to God in the Mystery of Christ. It is Christ Who is our Heaven, not the Cross. The Cross without Christ would be Hell—just as suffering, for those who do not know Christ, is always Hell.

4. "When Israel came out of Egypt"

Christ in the Psalter is our rock in the desert of Sinai. The Psalms, written and quickened by His Spirit, feed us with bread in the wilderness. They slake us (as Isaias says) at the Saviour's fountains!

We find Him by recognizing both Him and ourselves in the sufferings of David, of Israel. This recognition like a spark, kindles a flame. The spark is faith, and the flame love. This true love is charity. Charity is the fire of the Holy Spirit and the Spirit is the Spirit of Christ, the Spirit of God. In this one flame we are united to God in Christ. The experience of this flame is an experience of union, first with Christ suffering, then with Christ in glory. For, as St John of the Cross says, it is the same flame that first attacks our selfishness as its implacable enemy, then when selfishness is gone, rewards our love by flooding it with glory. [67]

But at the same time, our growth in Christ is measured not only by intensity of love but also by the deepening of our vision, for we begin to see Christ now not only in our own deep souls, not only in the Psalms, not only in the Mass, but everywhere, shining to the Father in the features of men's faces. The more we are united to Him in love the more we are united in love to one another, because there is only one charity embracing both God and our brother.

In this union we discover, and the conviction gains more and more power as we are emptied of selfishness by suffering, that there is so to speak "One mystical Person," after all, chanting the Psalms. It is now no longer we alone who pronounce the words of David or of some long dead Jew. It is the eternal Christ. He is "chanting the Psalms in heaven," because His glorified Humanity is the center of their Mysteries and the life of all who enter into these mysteries. All we who are members of His Body are one in Him and one with Him. His Church and bride is one with Him, according to the Apostle, "two in one flesh." And St Augustine comments: "Thus of these two (the Church and Christ) there is made as it were *one Person* . . . If they are two in one flesh, why not also *two in one voice?* Let Christ then speak, for in Christ the Church speaks and in the Church speaks Christ. The Head speaks in the Body and the Body in the Head." [68]

III

SACRAMENTA

SCRIPTURARUM

It is not merely the solution of one man's problem that is achieved in the Psalms or in the Mystery of Christ. If in my chanting of the Psalms I arrive only at a sense of individual and personal fulfilment in Christ, a sense that does not reach out and embrace all the other members of the Body who find their fulfilment in Him, then I fall far short of the contemplation that the Psalter holds in store for those who give themselves entirely to its Mysteries. The One Man who suffers in the Psalms, who cries out to God in them and by God is heard, this One Man is the Whole Christ. The consolations and help that are sent from heaven through the Psalms are poured out not simply on Jesus and myself but upon the Whole Christ, and I will find their strength far less potent in my own regard if I do not realize that they are shared among us all. It is a relatively small thing to awaken, in the recitation of a Psalm, to my own personal sonship of God. Far more marvelous is the greater consolation of the Mystery of my oneness with all the other sons of God in the One Son of God, the Mystical Christ. "The sons of God," says St Augustine, "are the body of the only Son of God; and since He is the Head and we the members, there is but One Son of God. Therefore he who loves the sons of God, loves the Son of God and he who loves the Son of God loves the Father. Nor can anyone love the Father unless he loves the Son; and whoever loves the Son must also love the sons of God . . . And by loving he himself becomes a member in the union of the Body of Christ and there shall be One Christ loving Himself." [69]

The secret of our fulfilment, then, is charity. We bring to the Psalms the raw material of our own poor, isolated persons, with our own individual conflicts and sufferings and trials. We throw them all into the fire of Christ's Love—or, if you prefer it, into the furnace of the Holy Spirit. In those flames we are purified of everything that isolates us, everything that is merely private, merely our own, and we are melted down to become a "new creature" with a new identity, a higher "personality." The discovery of our true selves, our own inviolable and individual beings united without confusion in this One Mystical Person, united to one another in the flame of Christ's infinite and selfless ecstasy of Love for His Father and for us, will constitute one of the purest perfections of our joy in heaven. Meanwhile, our recital of the Psalms should be a constant and progressive discovery of this Person who we all are. *Debemus intelligere Personam nostram, Personam Ecclesiae nostrae, Personam Corporis Christi.* "We must understand our Person, the Person of our Church, the Person of the Body of Christ." These are the words of St Augustine. [70]

4. "When Israel came out of Egypt"

This will help us to understand the importance of the Choral recitation of the Divine Office. The mere fact of standing in choir and of hearing twenty or thirty or fifty or a hundred voices all blending into one voice, crying out to God in the first person singular, is a great help toward realizing the truth we have just tried to set down.

We all differ, we all have our own problems and troubles, and yet we all sing together : "O God, hear *my* cry, hearken to *my* prayer . . ." The very syntax makes us one. And when we add : "From the ends of the earth *I cry* to thee," [71] our vision goes out to embrace the whole Mystical Body, in all its scattered members in every part of the world. And wherever they may be, those men and women are also here, and we are there with them, because we are all "one Man." Wherever two or three are gathered together in His Name, Christ, in the midst of them, imparts to them His identity. He becomes the "I" who sings and prays and praises in us all.

III

SACRAMENTA

SCRIPTURARUM

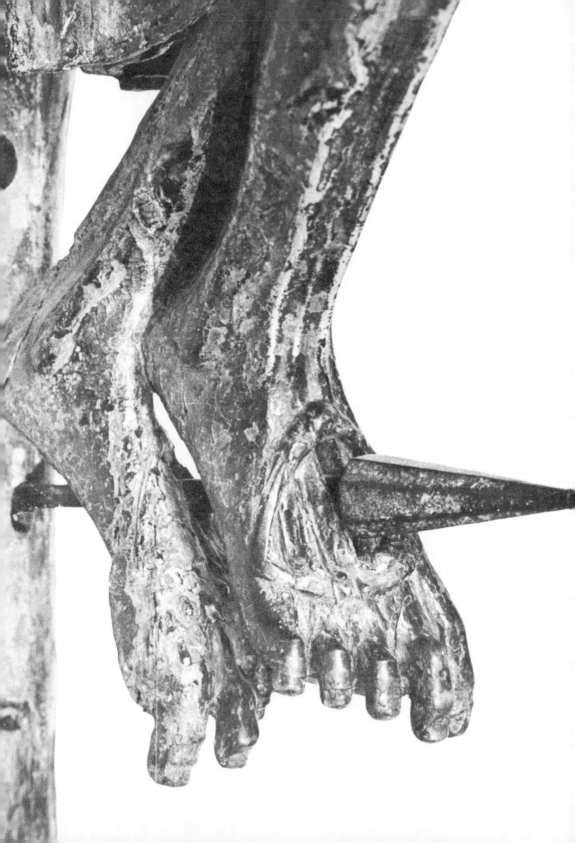

THE PERFECT LAW OF LIBERTY

IV

$$\mathbf{1:}$$

"Thou hast opened my ears . . ."

THE "GRADUAL PSALMS" ARE THOSE WHICH some suppose to have been sung by Jewish pilgrims on their way to celebrate the great feasts of the old Law in the City of David. [72] They are the shortest of the Psalms but not the least moving. St Augustine finds in them an expression of the joy of the Pilgrim Church on earth ascending to the Celestial Jerusalem. But, in a sense, all the Psalms are "gradual Psalms." They are the chants that lighten the fatigue of our journey homeward from the long exile of sin. Even when they are sorrowful, their very sorrow holds a hidden promise of beatitude, for "blessed are they that mourn." [73] This peculiar sorrow of the third beatitude, the sorrow of the soul that realizes its exile and can no longer find any consolation save in longing for home, is the beginning of our liberation. It teaches us the way to freedom by teaching us the truth that St Augustine expressed in six words: *Nisi beatus non vivit ut vult.* "Only the blessed live as they please." And he adds four more words that distinguish liberty from licence: *Nemo beatus nisi justus.* "No one is blessed un-less he first be just." This sentence from The *City of God* [74] should be taken as a corollary of his famous aphorism, "Love God and do what you will," which is as much as to say that if everything we do is an act of love for God, we will be free, because we will be unable to sin. Sin is captivity and love is liberty.

The Psalms teach us the way back to Paradise. Christ died that we might recover all that Adam lost in Eden, and more besides. What had Adam in Eden? This is not the place to study all his gifts and prerogatives. Let us think only, for the moment, of his blessed-ness, which was his liberty. But his blessedness and liberty were rooted in the possession of God. That possession was the work of love, uniting His will with the will of God, and of vision, filling His intellect with God. "Man lived just as he pleased in Paradise," says St Augus-tine, "as long as he willed what God commanded. His whole life was fruition of God, and by the possession of this infinite Good, Adam himself was made good." *Vivebat fruens Deo, ex quo bono erat bonus.* [75]

Indeed the Psalms not only show us the way back to Paradise, they are themselves a Paradise. In them the truth and love of God are not only shown to us but communicated to us in the Mystery of Christ, if we can only receive them. The Mystery of the Psalter is above all the Mystery of God's will: the history of Israel is a history of trial and suffering not so much because of the enemies of God's people, still less because Israel was forsaken by God, but because, of all things, Israel kept forsaking God by disobeying His will and mistrusting His Providence. The prevarication of the Chosen people is answered and the problems it causes are solved by the obedience of the Redeemer who comes to do God's will. "... But thou hast opened my ears. Burnt-offering and sin-offering thou didst not require. Then I said; 'Behold I come, in the volume of the book it is written of me: I delight to do thy will, O my God, and thy law is in the depths of my heart.'" [76]

"Thou hast opened my ears," says Christ in the Psalm. That is to say, "Thou hast made me perfectly obedient to the inspirations of Thy Spirit." "Thy Law is in the depths of my heart." St Bernard of Clairvaux knew what this Law was, because he was a contemplative and a saint. And to be a saint means to live by that Law, to be formed by it, and to be transformed by it and perfectly united to God.

Let us meditate a little on this mysterious "Law" since it is the secret of sanctity and of contemplation and since it is also the secret of the Psalter, hidden in the very center of the Mystery of Christ.

In the first place, this Law must not be understood as the Law of Moses, the "law of fear." The "Law" that is in the "depths of the heart" of the saint is not a law that paralyzes love. It is not and can never be a narrow, exterior religiosity, concentrated on the literal fulfilment of external precepts, a law that merely weighs and measures sins in the balance of a pitiless scrupulosity. St Paul travelled all over the Roman Empire to tell people that they had been delivered forever from such a law. "If you are led by the Spirit," he said, "you are not under the Law . . . For you have been called unto liberty." [77] But he immediately added that if they were unable to tell the difference between liberty and lawlessness, they would fall under the dominion of a far more terrible law, the law of the flesh. "Make not liberty an occasion for the flesh. . . for the flesh lusteth against the Spirit and the spirit against the flesh, and these two are contrary to one another *so that you do not the things that you would.*" [78]

IV

THE PERFECT

LAW OF LIBERTY

There are, then, three laws in the New Testament: first, the law of the flesh, the tyranny of passion, binding the soul of man to the treadmill of lust and hatred and greed and cruelty like blind Samson in Gaza; for the liberty of the flesh makes slaves. But the Law of Moses although it set itself up against the tyranny of the flesh, was not able to liberate any man from the flesh. Under the Old Law, man fell under a double tyranny. He was bound by one law of sin and by another law that accused him of sin and punished him for sin and imposed a weary burden of practices to expiate sin: and yet there was not one of these ablutions or sacrifices that could cleanse him of sin or deliver him from passion. Still the Old Law was not evil, for it had its function: it was the "type" of another Law, and its sacrifices foreshadowed the Mystery in which men would at last recover liberty. The Old Law was a gradual "education" and preparation for the liberty of the New. The Law of Moses was good not in itself but in its fulfilment, "For the end of the Law is Christ," [79] and "love is the fulfilling of the Law." [80]

It is of this third Law that St James speaks when he says: "He that hath looked into the perfect Law of liberty and hath continued therein, not becoming a forgetful hearer but a doer of the work, this man shall be blessed in his deed." [81] The Law of Christ is the Law of liberty because it is the Law of love—which is to say that it is above all law, since love, being free, knows no compulsion.

That is why St Bernard says that the saint is neither bound by law nor without law: *non sub lege nec sine lege*. What is the solution of this paradox? It is this. The Law of love is a law in the sense that it is a standard, but it is not a law in the sense of a limitation. It is an ideal but it is not a restriction: for love has no limits. We are called to love God without measure and for no other reason than that He is God. [82]

To love Him thus is to love Him as He loves Himself. To do so perfectly is to be transformed into Him, because it is to live by the same "Law" that rules the interior life of God. But that Law is not a law: it is a Person. It is Charity, the Holy Spirit. By virtue of this "Law" the Three Divine Persons cannot be anything but One, and they cannot be anything but infinitely happy. For God, infinite love, freedom and peace are compulsory. He is all these things and cannot

1. "Thou hast opened my ears"

wish to be otherwise. The saints, too, when they live by the same Law, as God, possess everything that He is. This, says St Bernard, is the "immaculate law of God" that we read of in the Psalms and which transforms souls. [83]

Charity is the only power, the only "Law" that can effect this mystical transformation. No other force can elevate us above our own nature. Charity is our only deliverance from human limitations. Note that I say charity and not love, for there is an immense distinction between them.

Love is a movement of the will toward what the intellect sees to be good. I speak only of spiritual love here. Sensual love is a movement of the will, guided by the senses, seeking their own satisfaction. There is a desire of God that is called charity although it remains a love for God as the highest good I can desire for myself. The desire for my own fulfilment in God, can be charity : but it must be educated and formed. For charity is the love of God, not precisely as my own highest good, but because He is good in Himself.

The highest and most perfect fruition of God is found in a love that rests in Him purely for His own sake alone. This love follows from the vision of Him as He is in Himself. I can and should desire this vision and love as my own highest good. Every Christian must, in fact, have something of the theological virtue of hope, which is explicitly directed towards this end : the fruition of God in heaven.

This is the great paradox of charity : that unless we are selfish enough to desire to become perfectly unselfish, we have not charity. And unless we love ourselves enough to seek perfect happiness in the total forgetfulness of ourselves, we will never find happiness. Charity is a self-interest which seeks fulfilment in the renunciation of all its interests. If I have charity I will seek my highest good in God, but I will find it in Him, not by taking Him to myself but by sacrificing myself for love of Him. And when my charity is thus perfect, I shall find and possess myself in Him.

As long as I am on earth, this paradox can serve as matter for discussion. In heaven, the vision of God disposes of the problem. St Thomas and Duns Scotus no longer need to argue, there, about the nature of charity and of blessedness. When we see Him, there will

IV

THE PERFECT

LAW OF LIBERTY

be no question of our loving anyone but Him. When we see Him, we will see that the only way to love any creature is to love God: for all creatures are meant to be loved in their Creator, and only in Him. We will see that it is only in Him that we can really love them: and that in thus loving them we are also loving Him. That is why St Bernard can say that we reach the highest degree of pure love when we finally love even ourselves in God and for His sake.

There too, love has ended in liberation. It has delivered us from complication, problem and paradox. There at last we arrive at the simplicity that God created us to have: for, after all, if He loves us, we cannot say we are not good, or that we are not to be loved. The perfection of love is a peak of unselfishness so lofty that it is above the stained atmosphere of this earth in which even humility and unselfishness have, in spite of all our good will, to suffer certain distortions. On that mountain top we are at last selfless enough to love God in ourselves without any need for comment or for excuse. For what we thus love is only His will in us. We love ourselves in the perfection to which He has brought us, not because we are perfect, not because we are happy, but because His will is done. And we are at last perfect, at last perfectly happy, because we no longer care whether or not we are perfect or happy. We simply find our peace in this: that in our souls, as in all else, His will is done. [84]

It is clear that this love is the fulfilment of the law because it is the perfect fulfilment of the will of God. Such love as this, when it is found on earth, fulfils every smallest detail of the most minute rubric of the Liturgy, every jot and tittle of its religious rule and its other obligations, not in a spirit of hair-splitting Pharisaism but with the freedom of a child of God to whom these things are no longer a matter of compulsion but a source of joy: and that is why the just man needs no law. This too is the explanation of Christ's words that He came not to destroy the Law of Moses, but to fulfil it. [85] Only this love can satisfy Christ's injunction that our justice must abound beyond that of the Scribes and Pharisees. [86]

St Bernard knew that such perfection of love was a kind of ecstasy. And he found it everywhere in the Psalms. This pure and ecstatic love, this love which is the mystical marriage of the soul with God,

1. *"Thou hast opened my ears"*

is what is meant by the word "justice" in the line, "Thy justice is as the mountains of God." [87] This love is the *mons coagulatus, mons pinguis* of the Vulgate version of Psalm 67 (the new translation calls it a "high-ridged and wooded mountain.") This pure and mystical love, continues St Bernard, is the mountain of God in Psalm 23— where the Psalmist asks: "Who can go up to the mountain of the Lord?" It is therefore the term of the ascetic life that is outlined in the middle of the Psalm:

Who can go up to the mountain of the Lord or who shall stand in his holy place?

He that has clean hands and a pure heart, who does not set his mind on vain things, and has not sworn deceitfully to his neighbor.

He shall receive a blessing from the Lord and mercy from God his Saviour.

This is the generation of them that seek him, of them that seek the face of the God of Jacob. [88]

IV

THE PERFECT

LAW OF LIBERTY

This same Psalm is one of the cornerstones of monastic spirituality, since it has an important place in the Prologue to St Benedict's Rule. It is therefore interesting to see how much a monastic saint like Bernard of Clairvaux could find in it. A detailed commentary of the apparently prosaic little virtues mentioned in these two or three lines would reveal that the Fathers believed "purity of heart" to be a function of that gift of understanding which is one of the keys to mystical contemplation. [89]

2:

From Praise to Ecstasy

IF, AS THE FATHERS TELL US, THIS PURE AND ECSTATIC love for God, which flows from a knowledge of God as He is in Himself, is the secret of contemplation, and if the Psalms are everywhere full of this love, then it is clear that the Psalter is a school of contemplation which has no equal except the Gospels and St Paul. Yet, in a certain sense, the Psalms have an accidental advantage over the New Testament. We *pray* them. We chant them together. They form part of an action into which the whole Church enters, and in that action, that prayer, the Spirit of Love Who wrote the Psalms and Who communicates Himself to us in them, works on us all and raises us up to God. To make the Psalms a preparation for contemplative prayer we must do all that we can to pray them with pure minds and pure hearts, living out their meaning with a charity that praises God as they praise Him. There is no purer praise of God than we find in the Psalms. If we make that purity our own, we lay ourselves open as targets, which fire from heaven can strike and consume : and this is all our desire, and God's desire for us.

The spirit of praise which is that of the Psalms is nothing else but the ecstatic love for God because He is God. Over and over again their inspired verses echo with the refrain : *confitemini Domino quoniam bonus.* "Give praise to the Lord because He is good, and because His mercy endureth for ever." To praise God thus, says St Bernard, simply because He is good in Himself, is to live by the "law of charity which is the law of His sons." [90]

When King Solomon dedicated the Temple of Jerusalem to God it is written that the Levites and the people lifted up their voices to praise God, singing the Psalms and chanting, "Give praise to the Lord for He is good" and immediately the "house of God was filled with a cloud." [91] This cloud was the sign of the presence of God, as we read in many places in *Exodus,* and it has become the traditional symbol of mystical contemplation. So too when we, in the temple of our souls, chant pure praise to God in the words of His Psalms, we can hope that He will fill us with this gift of His obscure and pacifying presence which is the first sign of infused contemplation. He will do so when our love for Him is sufficiently pure to exclude every other affection.

The echo of this refrain, *confitemini Domino quoniam bonus* resounds in all the pages of the Old Testament where are recorded the triumphs of Israel over the enemies of God's people. They are the song of a people united to their God as He intended them to be, putting all their trust in Him not only because He is good, but because He alone is good. This ecstasy of praise sums up the mysticism of the Old Testament and of David above all. And its echo is the living flame of those Psalms which, grouped together in the *Hallel,* first kindled the new fire which was to be the Liturgy of our Mass. Therefore, this praise of God "because He is good and because His mercy endureth forever" has passed over, with all the transfigured symbols and types of the Old Testament, into the New. The song that resounded on the shores of the Red Sea and shone on the dark desert in Israel's tents, burst from the Sepulchre with Christ, clad in a new and invisible splendor, and ascended with Him from Olivet into heaven where it is at once the vision, the love, the praise of all the blessed.

IV

THE PERFECT

LAW OF LIBERTY

This mystical love is not only a song of victory in the sense that it follows and celebrates all our victories, but also in the sense that by itself alone it has power to overthrow our spiritual enemies and to put victory in our hands. It is because the Church is always singing it, that the gates of hell cannot prevail against her. But if they sometimes seem to prevail, it is perhaps because those members of the Church's fighting army whose task it is to sing these Psalms on earth, do not have the light or the purity to enter into their spirit. They cannot hurl down her enemies at once because they form the words on their lips without realizing and without living the pure love which is their meaning.

It was not so on the day when King Josaphat prayed to God, and, guided by the voice of a prophet, led the army of Juda out against Moab and Ammon and Seir with singers at their head and Levites chanting and blowing trumpets in the desert:

And they rose early in the morning, and went out through the desert of Thecua: and as they were marching, Josaphat, standing in the midst of them, said: "Hear me, ye men of Juda and all the inhabitants of Jerusalem:

108

*believe in the Lord your God and you shall be secure: believe His prophets
and all things shall succeed well." And he gave counsel to the people and
appointed the singing men of the Lord to praise Him by their companies and to
go before the army and with one voice to say: "Give glory to the Lord, for His
mercy endureth for ever."* [92] The Scriptures go on to tell us what happened. While Juda sang in the desert, the armies of Moab and Ammon
rose up against their allies from Mount Seir and slaughtered them.
Then they turned upon one another in their camp "And when Juda
came to the watch tower that looketh toward the desert, they saw
afar off all the country for a great space full of dead bodies, and that
no one was left that could escape death."[93]

So too will it be one day with the Church, when her Levites have
entered into the simplicity of the Psalms and have found in them their
strength, who is their Christ, and have lost themselves in contemplation and in the pure love of God against which there is no prevailing:
for those who taste the fruits of the Spirit come under no law. [94]

To chant the Psalms in such a spirit is to join in the Liturgy of
heaven. It is to praise God with something of the same love with
which He is praised by the blessed spirits. Tradition, in fact, everywhere points out that the monastic life brings the monk into close
participation with the angels and saints of heaven. They are all one in
the heavenly city by virtue of the pure love that unites them in God.
It is therefore this charity most of all that is demanded of us when
we go to choir to chant the Psalms.

2. From Praise to Ecstasy

St Augustine's commentary on Psalm 53 contains a passage that
can fittingly serve as a summary to all that we have been saying about
the liberty of the sons of God which is the reward of pure love and
which opens paradise to us even while we remain in exile here
below.

What is the Mystery of the fifty-third Psalm? It is sung by David
after his deliverance by God from the hands of Saul. David — the
type of Christ and therefore a personification of the Mystical Christ
and of each member of that Christ — has fled with six hundred men
from Ceila, and now "he abode in the deserts in strongholds and
remained in a mountain in the desert of Ziph, in a woody hill." [95]
David hiding in the forests of Ziph, says St Augustine, is Christ hid-

den in the desert of this world. The Ziphites represent those who do not recognize the chosen one of God in one who has no temporal power and who has to flee before the face of Saul, the prince of this world. In their contempt for the Holy One they seek to betray Him to Saul, and they send messengers to the king in Gabaa, saying "Lo, doth not David lie hid with us in the strongholds of the wood in mount Hacila, which is on the right hand of the desert?" Saul sends them back to follow David's movements while he prepares a force of men to encircle David and trap him in the forest. David hears of this, and moves with his guerillas to the wilderness of Maon. There Saul catches up with him and surrounds him. David's situation is so desperate that he sees no human hope of salvation, but just then a messenger comes and informs Saul that the Philistines have invaded his kingdom, so that he retires, with his army, and David is saved. Psalm 53 gives both David's prayer for help and his thanksgiving to God when the prayer is answered. The whole story is telescoped in the short Psalm in which the prayer and its answer are immediately joined together without transition because when the Church prays she is already answered.

IV

THE PERFECT

LAW OF LIBERTY

"Behold," sings David, "God helps me; the Lord is the support of my life . . . I will freely sacrifice to thee; I will praise thy name, O Lord, for it is good." [96]

The line that concerns us most is this one: *Voluntarie sacrificabo tibi*. "I will freely sacrifice to thee." What is the meaning of this word "freely"? We have by this time seen something of the theology of Christian freedom, which is the spiritual freedom of pure and ecstatic love, perfected in the union of the soul with God in contemplation and mystical union. St Augustine asks, "Who can understand this spiritual gift (*hoc bonum cordis*) when another speaks of it, if he has not first himself tasted it in himself?" And he goes on to explain it, saying that those who know it by experience will understand his words, and that those who have not experienced this pure love should pray to do so in order that they too might know what it is.

The perfection of sacrifice, says St Augustine, is found in the freedom that makes sacrifice gratuitous and pure. This purity although it does not reflect upon itself, does not consider its own interests, is not, nevertheless, without its reward. It is its own reward. This pure praise, this "free sacrifice," consists then in praising God not merely because we are delighted with the favors He has granted or will grant us, but because we are delighted with Him, the giver of all gifts. And this delight is situated in the praise itself. We rejoice in praising Him because praise itself is our joy. *Gratis amo quod laudo. Laudo Deum et in ipsa laude gaudeo.* [97]

If we praised God merely for the sake of obtaining something from Him, then our praise would be contingent upon a gift of His. It would therefore be dependent upon an uncertainty, for although God will never fail to answer all our prayers, He will not necessarily give us precisely the thing we ask of Him. If our praise depends, then, on an uncertainty, it is bound by a restriction. And if it is restricted, the heart with which we pray to God will also be narrowed and limited by the restriction imposed upon us by our own desire, which is centered upon something less than the infinite God. Therefore our praise will not be perfectly "free." It will be fettered, it will be imprisoned by the limitations of our own heart But we cannot give God perfect praise and sacrifice if we remain the captives of our own insignificance. "How shall we sing the song of the Lord in a strange land?" [98]

2. *From Praise to Ecstasy*

That is why we so often find ourselves chanting our Psalter by the waters of Babylon instead of on the towers of Sion. No wonder our Office is not contemplation. We have hung up our harps "on the willows of that land," that is to say, we have suspended our prayer upon the stunted branches of human desires. Our contemplation is something grey and dusty. It hangs inert upon a pale green thing with shallow roots in the mud of a jaundiced river. It shines in a heart that is not the wide-open mirror of heaven but a sandy prison of human hopes, centered on transient things.

"If you praise God in order that He may give you something that is not Himself," says St Augustine, "you do not love Him freely. You would blush if your wife loved you for your money. If perchance, you were to become poor, she might look about for some other partner! Well, if you want your wife to love you freely, for what you are, why do you love God for something other than Himself?'' [99]

This lesson has a subtler application than the reader may think. I am passing over those whose main intention, in praying to God, has to do with health, pleasure, or money. There is nothing the matter with such an intention. It is quite true that we are meant to ask God for everything we need, for God has ordered us to do so. But there is a perfect way of so praying, which rests in God and not in our temporal intention.

IV

THE PERFECT

LAW OF LIBERTY

THE SHADOW OF THY WINGS

V

1:

Dark Lightning

CONTEMPLATION, IS A GIFT OF GOD, IN WHICH THE soul, purified by His infused love, suddenly and inexplicably experiences the presence of God within itself. This experiential recognition of God springs from the fact that pure charity has reformed the likeness to God which makes our soul like a mirror created only to reflect Him. Because contemplation is produced through the grace of an intimate union with Christ, Who is the Son of God by nature, it is essentially a full and mature participation of His divine Sonship. In contemplation, we know God formally as our "Father," that is to say not only as our Creator in the natural order, but as the living and intimately active source of our supernatural life as well. Contemplation is our personal response to His mystical presence and activity within us. We suddenly realize that we are confronted with the infinitely rich source of all Being and all Love, and although we do not literally "see" Him, for our meeting takes place in the dark night of faith, yet there is something in the deepest center of our being, something at the very spiritual apex of our life, that leaps with elation at this contact with the Being of Him who is almighty. The spark that is struck within us by this touch of the finger of God kindles a sheet of flame that goes forth to proclaim His presence in every fibre of our being and to praise Him from the marrow of our bones.

Generally speaking, this "experiential recognition" of God by the contemplative, takes place on two different levels. When Jesus met the two Disciples on the road to Emmaus, on the afternoon of the first Easter Sunday, "their eyes were held and they did not know Him," but nevertheless "their heart was burning within them whilst He spoke to them in the way and opened to them the Scriptures." But when they reached the village of their destination and Jesus, pressed by their ardent love, sat down to break bread with them, "their eyes were opened and they knew Him and He vanished out of their sight." [100] The first of these recognitions suggests to us the common experience of what is called "living faith." The second offers a good analogy for mystical contemplation properly so-called. [101]

Although faith is formally in the intellect, it is nevertheless a perception of God that is impregnated with affectivity. On the one hand the God we attain by faith is at the same time infinite Truth and infinite Love, and on the other, the faith that attains to Him is an act of the intellect moved by the loving will. In actual fact, then, "living faith" is a faith that obscurely responds to the reality of God by a movement of love. Faith is penetrated with love. It only establishes a living contact between the soul and God in so far as it is vitalized by charity. But the more intense is the love that moves us to seek God beneath the analogical formulas of revealed truth, the more vital will be the grasp of our faith upon the hidden reality of God. So, in the experience of living faith our "eyes are held" in so far as the intellect is in darkness and assents without intrinsic evidence to the truths proposed to us. We do not realize how close God is to us, and yet our "hearts burn within us" because of the ardor of our love.

V

THE SHADOW

OF THY WINGS

This ardor of love constitutes a kind of indirect experience of God. The interior soul, without yet realizing how much this experience can mean, becomes aware, by a kind of ingenuous reflection upon this burning of love, that this must be a sign or an effect of the presence of God. And thus it seeks Him with a more or less conscious and enlightened ardor in the pages of Scripture and especially in the prayers of the Liturgy and the verses of the Psalms. Such a person soon finds that there is hardly a line in the Office, hardly a word in the Mass, that is not capable at one time or another of awakening this interior burning of love that mutely betrays the fact that God is close at hand. This "living faith" then becomes habitual. It transforms the Office from a routine into a constant joy. Living faith prepares us for contemplation. The experience I have just described is not contemplation in the strict sense. It is only a "masked" or "veiled" contemplation — one that is not fully developed or consciously aware of its own potentialities. Nevertheless, it is quite sufficient to make the recital of the Office contemplative in a broad sense. It enlivens our choral prayer with frequent "recognitions" of God in His inspired words, it trains us to sense His comings and goings in our own heart, it gives us eyes that penetrate into the deepest meanings of the Psalms and brings us under the intimate guidance of the Holy Spirit, who is ever anxious to lead us on to a deeper and deeper penetration of the mysteries of our Redemption. Finally, these movements of obscure and loving faith soon gain a hold over our minds and wills. If we are quick to respond to them, we find that they lovingly retain us and hold us, for long, thoughtless moments, under their spell. Thus we quite easily and spontaneously come to spend much of the time of our Office in these smooth flights of simple repose, gliding through the verses of the Psalms with our hearts absorbed in a simple gaze upon the God Who is invisible but near, and Whose love now holds us captive by its unworldly charm.

But it also happens — and this is rarer — that under the pressure of a very great love, or in the darkness of a conflict that exacts a heroic renunciation of our whole self, or in the ecstasy of a sudden splendid joy that does not belong to this earth, the soul will be raised out of itself. It will come face to face with the Christ of the Psalms. In an experience that might be likened to a flash of dark lightning, a thunderclap on the surface of the abyss, "its eyes will be opened and it will know Him and He will vanish from its sight." [102] This *1. Dark Lightning* momentary blaze of recognition is not produced by a created species or image in the soul. It is the flash of a flame that is touched off by an immediate contact of the substance of the soul with God Himself. In one terrific second that belongs not to time but to eternity the whole soul is transfixed and illumined by the tremendous darkness which is the light of God. And from the heart of that darkness speaks the voice of the eternal Christ, and now, although we still cannot be said to "see," we experience in all truth what before we only believed, and we "know" that He is the Son of God, the King of Glory, and that "He is in the Father and we are in Him and He is in us." [103]

It is sometimes given to a soul, in an experience of love that is absolutely terrible, to enter deeply into the mystery of Christ's Passion as it is presented to us by the Holy Spirit, in the Psalms. At such a moment, one can experience something of what St Paul spoke of. The text of his which I have in mind is the keynote of the Holy Week Liturgy, since it opens the Epistle for Palm Sunday, is repeated at the Gradual of Holy Thursday, and recurs over and over again in the antiphon of all the canonical hours from Holy Thursday to the Holy Saturday: " *Let this mind be in you which was also in Christ Jesus, who, being in the form of God, thought it not robbery to be equal with God; but emptied Himself taking the form of a servant . . . He humbled Himself becoming obedient unto death, even the death of the Cross.* For which cause God hath exalted Him and hath given Him a name that is above all names. . ." [104]

Hoc enim sentite in vobis. Perhaps the old expression, "let this mind be in you," does not quite convey to us all that St Paul means. We are to experience what Christ experienced. The same thing has to happen to us. We have to live through it. Or rather, Christ has to live through it again *in us.* And what does He have to live through? This *emptying,* this total outpouring of ourselves, until we too have to cry *Consummatum est!* "Round about me are many bulls, the strong bulls of Basan hem me in. They open their mouth against me like a lion ravening and roaring. I am poured out like water, and all my bones are disjointed: my heart has become like wax, it melts in my bowels. My throat is dried up like a potsherd and my tongue cleaves to my jaws; thou hast brought me down to the dust of death . . . . [105]

V

THE SHADOW

OF THY WINGS

It can sometimes happen that we too are brought down by Christ's love, into the dust of death. Then we know, somewhat as He knew, what it is to be " poured out like water." It is the terrible experience of seeing oneself slowly turned inside out. It is the frightful taste of a humility that is not merely a virtue but the very agony of truth. This ghastly emptying, this inexorable gutting of our own appalling nonentity, takes place under the piercing light of the revealed word, the light of infinite Truth. But it is something far more terrible still: we find ourselves eviscerated by our own ingratitude, under the eyes of Mercy.

This is the experience that will come to one who once thought he had virtue, who once thought he had a "degree of prayer," who once thought, perhaps, that he loved God indeed, and was God's good friend and who then, one day, is brought up for judgment, to be purified of all that is too human in his dream. For he has been cornered and accused, pierced and emptied by the shame of remembering who he really is. God seems to turn away His face. God seems to withdraw His protecting hand, and all the things he treasured, that were not God, have wasted away like shadows with the loss of His presence. This emptiness, this sense of spiritual annihilation which is due to us all as men born in sin and grown old in sin, Christ took upon Himself when it was not due to Him at all and He emptied Himself of all His power and glory in order to descend into the freezing depths of darkness where we had crawled to hide ourselves, cowering in blind despair.

But because Christ came down into this no-man's land of sin, to find us and bring us back to His Kingdom, we are able to discover the living God in the very darkness of what seems to be His utter absence. And what is more, it may be that we find Him there more truly than when we thought we saw Him in the light of our own dim day.

So it can happen that a soul enters upon the recital of a Psalm applicable to Christ's Passion—let us say Psalm 87. It is a day on which we seem to be buried alive under an inhuman burden of temptation. Perhaps we may also suffer sickness, physical as well as moral desolation. But the worst thing of all remains the inescapable vision of our own almost infinite capacity for pettiness and degradation. "O Lord my God, I cry by day, in the night I weep before thee. Let my prayer come before thee, incline thy ear to my cry. For my soul is full of evils and my life is on the verge of the grave . . . Thou hast laid me in a deep pit, in darkness, in the abyss. Thine indignation weighs upon me and with all thy waves thou dost overwhelm me. Thou hast taken away my friends from me; thou hast made me abominable to them; I am shut up, I can no longer go forth." [106] This is practically the only Psalm that ends on a note of complete dejection. There is a faint flame of hopeful prayer, but it is beaten down by the cold darkness of apparent refusal, and here is how the Psalm ends: "Thy wrath has swept over me and thy terrors have destroyed me. They surround me like water all the time: they assail me all together. Thou hast taken from me friend and companion; The darkness is my intimate." And that is all.

1. Dark Lightning

Yet at such a moment, and in such a Psalm, the soul, catching and comprehending in its own black mirror the fearful darkness of revelation, is confronted in its own depths with the countenance of the murdered Christ. This is more than a meeting. It is an identification. We have entered into a Baptism of darkness in which we are one with His death. But to die with Christ is to rise with Him, for we cannot be dead with Him without our life being hidden with Him in God. [107] Although there remains a formal difference between the grace of the Passion of Christ by which we are delivered from sin, and the grace of His Resurrection in which supernatural life is communicated to us, nevertheless in fact both are poured out in the wonderful night of which the Liturgy sings in the *Exultet*. [108] This night of Mystery in which we rise from death with the hidden Christ is the spiritual Red Sea of which the Psalms have sung to us all along. Now we have entered into it in truth and have passed through it to be nourished by God with His Body in the wilderness.

V

THE SHADOW
OF THY WINGS

This is a death in which we have found Him Who is the way, the truth and the life. We now know that this darkness, which seems to annihilate us, is not the darkness of death but, if such an expression can be understood, the darkness of life. The tides of light that pour down upon the whole Church from the mountain top which is the soul of the Risen Saviour, blind us by their intense purity and drown us in darkness although they are essential Light, and so the Night of the Spirit is already a sharing of the Resurrection. If the paradox may be allowed, this frightful death is our first taste of glory.

Then we begin to discover that the night in which we seem to be lost is the protection of the shadow of God's wings. [109] If God has brought us into this darkness it is because He wishes to guard us with extreme care and tenderness, or, in the words of the Psalm, "like the apple of His eye." [110] The new life of the soul united Christ in His Mystery is something too delicate and tender to be let loose in a crowd that may contain hidden enemies, and therefore God has isolated the soul in a soundless and vast interior solitude, the solitude of His own Heart where there is no human spectator and where the soul can no longer even see itself. True, the depths of that solitude open and close in a flash: but the soul remains enveloped and penetrated with divine emptiness, saturated with the vastness of God, charged with the living voice of silence in which His Word is eternally uttered.

The protection of darkness and silence is extremely necessary for the soul that begins to burn with these touches of the Spirit of God. If it should come close to Him Who is Life without being enclosed and hidden in His life, it will find itself charged with more power than it can stand and it will burn itself out with an ardor that it cannot control. For when the soul has thus known God divinely, the memory of the encounter is sometimes stirred up by the lines of Psalms, to a blaze that unnerves it beyond its capacity to bear. In this degree of prayer there may arise high seas of inspiration that destroy the mind with the weight of a superhuman demand. But we have no help from God to tackle this demand. It is not the wave of His present power, but an undertow that follows after His passing. Caught in the clenched fist of this bullying sea of love that is neither human nor divine and which seems to be something elemental in its brutality, we are drawn under and seem to drown until God catches us again and holds us under, not under the sea but under the Mystery of His eternity, where alone there is breathing.

1. Dark Lightning

This undertow, too, flows through the Psalms. It tends to attack us most where there are appeals made to our mind and will by the word of God, by ceremony and liturgy and chant. These aids to prayer which were a help to us at the very beginning and which went unnoticed as we advanced in living faith and in the prayer of quiet, which were sources of light and brought us into intimate union with Christ in His Mysteries, now turn against us like Goliath and we have no stones and sling with which to fight back. This is the time when every line of the Psalms bursts forth with lights that we no longer need, spurious and tremendous inspirations that exhaust the soul and contribute nothing to its peace. And the soul seems to find no refuge where it may flee them. They come upon it like an army from every side and there is no resistance. The only safety is in darkness, the protection that can only be extended over us by the outstretched hand of God. We need that protection, and more and more we sense our need. For the devils too, understand our position. They stand to profit if they can destroy and exhaust us with false lights and raptures of their own devising. This is the stage when the soul that is too tough for its own good, too well able to stand the overpowering sweetness of halfnatural ecstasies, will be in danger of entering the ways of false mysticism. Prayer will become debauchery, the Liturgy a riot of prophecy and carnal exaltation. The mark of all this falsity is violence. It is sealed with the seal of contention and brutality and strain. These are the spiritual footprints of the devil who, if he cannot deceive the soul with false raptures, soon tears off his mask and lets loose against us a jungle full of terrors and we live in nightmare on the threshold of the deepest darkness that alone can save us.

In this tribulation the Lord God is ever with us, no matter how much we fear. *Cum ipso sum in tribulatione.* These are words from Psalm 90 which are chanted every night in the monastic Compline when the shadows fall upon the cloister and the monks are ending their day of prayer. "I will be with him in trouble, I will rescue him and honor him."[111] The angels are at our side, holding us up lest we should dash our foot against a stone. We could not travel through the forest that the spiritual life has now become, unless His power carried us onward, where we tread upon the asp and basilisk and never feel their sting, and never suffer harm! *Altissimum posuisti refugium tuum.* We have made the Most High God our refuge. The scourge will never touch us.

What are the horizons that lie ahead, in the ascent to the City of God in heaven? There are high peaks before us now, serene with snow and light, above the level of tempest. They are far away. We almost never see them they are so high. But we lift up our eyes toward them, for there the saints dwell: and these are the mountains of holiness whence cometh our help. *Levari oculos meos in montes unde veniet auxilium mihi.* [112]

V

THE SHADOW

OF THY WINGS

2:

The Silence of the Psalms

ONE THING REMAINS TO BE EXPLAINED. WE HAVE emphasized, in this book, the truth that the Psalms most often become contemplation when, through them, we manage to unite our sufferings with the sufferings of Christ, so that He in turn lifts us up in His own triumph and raises us to a foretaste of His glory. Why this emphasis on suffering? Suffering is not the only theme in the Psalter.

We bring the substance of our own lives to the Psalter and offer it to Christ to be transformed by Him. It is all matter for sacrifice. But since life on earth is what it is, we all have plenty of trouble, plenty of suffering, plenty of misery. We have our joys too. And we should not omit to offer them to Christ and unite them with His joys. But I insist on the importance of bringing Him our sufferings because it is precisely these that He wishes to transfigure into His purest joys. After all, the real joys of life do not come when we supernaturalize our trifling little human successes with an act of pure intention. We enter into true joy through the center of our own nothingness. We find true happiness by dying, because our truest happiness belongs to heaven and we can only enter heaven by dying to the things of earth. It is quite normal, then, that the theme of suffering in the Psalms should lend itself very readily to contemplative union because "through many tribulations we must enter into the Kingdom of God." [113]

But, finally, here is the deepest reason of all for the intimate connection between the Cross and contemplation. It is a theme that comes before us more than once in the Liturgy of Passiontide. Christ said "Unless the grain of wheat, falling into the ground, die, *itself remaineth alone.*" [114] It is by His Passion and death that Jesus gathers to His Heart the sons of God, those whom His Father has given Him, of whom not one shall be lost. It is "when He is lifted up that he draws all things to Himself." It is in His passion that He wins them all for His own, and earns the right to offer them all to His Father and raises them all into the life of grace and glory. It is by dying for us that Jesus has drawn us all into the triumph of His Resurrection. All this is set before us with a clarity that is as beautiful as it is terrifying, in the unwitting prophecy of the High Priest Caiphas: "It is expedient that one man should die for the people and that the whole nation perish not. And this he spoke not of himself, but being the high priest of that year he prophesied that Jesus should die for the nation, and not only for the nation, *but to gather together in one the children of God that were dispersed.*" [115]

That is why the Cross of Christ is the key to the Psalms. The Mystery of the Mystical Body, as St Augustine so often insisted, is central to the Psalter and essential for its proper use as prayer, and the texts we have just quoted show us the connection between the Cross and the Mystical Body. Hence it is from the tree of the Cross that all the other mysteries in the Psalter bud forth and spread out before the gaze of the contemplative, and once we have entered into the Mystery of Christ's Death, the Resurrection and Ascension into heaven are assured us. Indeed, since the Mystery of Christ's death is the Mystery of Unity of His Mystical Body, by entering into His death we are helping Him to "draw all things to Himself." When we are most intimately united with Him by love and hidden in the "secret of His Face" we are in the truest sense Apostles. [116] Those who exercise the greatest power, in the Communion of Saints, are those whom the Lord has "hidden in His tent from the wrangling of tongues." [117] I am not here talking of exterior silence or of a vocation to an enclosed Order, but of the interior silence of the mystic, in no matter what walk of life he may happen to find himself, for it may happen, and it should happen, that even one who has to preach and teach should remain protected from the inanity of vain speech, should keep His heart a sacred sanctuary for the word of God, hidden in the urn of contemplation like manna in the Ark. There is more than meets the eye in this Mystery which the Psalmist speaks of as the "wrangling of tongues."

The "wrangling of tongues" symbolizes the confusion that was sent down by God upon the builders of Babel, who, seeking to scale heaven with a structure of their own devising, were darkened and scattered in a division of tongues. [118] Babylon, the city of division, the city of those who "love themselves unto the hatred of God," [119] was born in a curse of tongues and the Church, the City of union, the City of those who love God unto hatred of themselves

V

THE SHADOW

OF THY WINGS

was born of the gift of tongues. The Holy Ghost was poured out at Pentecost in tongues of flame, and made the Apostles speak in all languages in order that men might be drawn back into union and that the division, laid open at Babel, might be closed again and healed in Christ and in His peace. For there is only one language spoken in the City of God. That language is charity. Those who speak it best, speak it in silence. For the eternal Word of Truth is uttered in silence. If He is uttered in silence, He must be heard in deepest silence. And His Spirit, the Spirit of Love, is also poured out into our hearts, proceeding from the Father and the Son, in an everlasting silence.

The Psalms are more than language. They contain within themselves the silence of high mountains and the silence of heaven. It is only when we stand at the bottom of the mountain that it is hard for us to distinguish the language of the Psalter from the tongues of this earth: for Christ must still perforce travel among us as a pilgrim disguised in our own tattered garments. The Psalter only truly begins to speak and sing within us when we have been led by God and lifted up by Him, and have ascended into its silences. When this is done, the Psalms themselves become the Tabernacle of God in which we are protected forever from the rage of the city of business, from the racket of human opinions, from the wild carnival we carry in our hearts and which the ancient saints called "Babylon."

2. The Silence of the Psalms

The Liturgy of Heaven is a most perfect harmony which, like the music of the spheres, sees song transfigured into silence. The Psalter is the prelude to that Liturgy. A prelude is a real beginning. We who chant the Psalms are standing in the courts of Heaven. That, indeed, is our chosen testimony. It is the Christian vocation: to begin on earth the life and Liturgy of Heaven. St John in his Apocalypse describes the songs of the four-and-twenty elders and of the blessed spirits. Their Liturgy is full of echoes of the Psalter. Theirs are the same themes for theirs is the perfect liberty which the Psalms foreshadow. They sing of the great mercy of God their liberator, and in doing so they burn with glory because they see and love Him as He really is. We have already entered with them but obscurely, into this Mystery. We have tasted the wine of their wedding feast paid out to us in droplets in moments of our own earthly Liturgy.

The wine of the Psalter and the wine of Heaven are the same, and they are ours, because whether in Heaven or on earth there is only one chalice, and that chalice itself is Heaven. It is the cup Jesus gave to His Disciples on the night when He said to them : " With desire have I desired to eat this Pasch with you." [120] There is one Mystery in the Kingdom of heaven, which is the light of that Kingdom, replacing the sun, moon and stars. It is the light also of the Psalter and of the Church on earth, though it shine in darkness. Its light is wine. It was of this wine that Jesus said: "I shall not drink the fruit of this vine again until I drink it with you now in the Kingdom of my Father." [121] He had just chanted the Psalms of the *Hallel* with His Apostles. He knew His Blood would flow like silence through our Psalter.

V

THE SHADOW

OF THY WINGS

"I WILL PRAY WITH THE SPIRIT" WROTE ST PAUL
to the Corinthians, "I will pray also with the understanding; I will
sing with the spirit, I will sing also with the understanding."[122]

So, too, when we sing the Psalms, the words that are placed before
us by the Church are supposed to awaken all the deepest powers of
our being and raise us up to God—or rather to show us that, because
of the death and Resurrection of Christ, we find ourselves at this very
moment *in* God, Whose Kingdom has come and is waiting to be
revealed in us His sons. How will it be revealed to the world unless
it first be realised in us, in whom the Scriptures are to be fulfilled?

The Spirit of God, pouring out the charity of God in our hearts,
makes us love the sanctity of God. He makes us reach out to receive
the gift of holiness which is offered to us in Christ by The Father's
infinite mercy. The deep fire of prayer which burns in the heart of
the Psalter is therefore a fire of sacrifice, the same fire which con-
sumed the Heart of Jesus Himself and brought Him to the Cross
for us, and brings us gladly and triumphantly down into the gates
of death for love of Him. This love, this chaste and selfless passion
that drives us out into the desert, seeking holiness in the renunciation of all things, this is the key to the understanding of the
Psalter because it is itself the fulfilment of the Psalter.

St Paul says that love is the fulfilment of the Law. Now the Old
Law as a whole is a type or figure of the New. The " spiritual
meaning " of the Old Law is therefore to be sought in the charity
which is the very substance of the New Testament. St Thomas points
out that the New Law is something more than a written document.
It is grace itself living and acting in the hearts of the faithful. It is
the Holy Spirit, present in the souls of those who have died together
with Christ and have risen with Him from the dead. The Angelic
Doctor quotes St Augustine, who says: "The Laws of God, written
in our hearts, are nothing else but the presence of the Holy Spirit
in us."[123]

Hence we may dare to say that charity, not as a pale abstraction
but as the flame breathed through our being by the presence and
action of the Holy Spirit, alone enables us to plumb the depths of
the "spiritual sense" of Scripture. What is hidden beneath the

133

literal meaning is not merely another and more hidden *meaning*, it is also a new and totally different *reality*: it is the divine life itself. This "meaning" of Scripture is never grasped if it is merely "known." It must be possessed and lived. God is not fully known when He is only "known" by the understanding. He is best known by us when He takes possession of our whole being and unites us to Himself. Then we know Him not in an idea but beyond ideas, in a contact of love, in an experience of Who He is, in a realization that He and He alone is our life and that without Him we are nothing. It is our joy to be nothing, and to know that He is all.

St Augustine long ago brought out this aspect of the distinction between "letter and spirit." He knew that Paul's phrase: "the letter killeth but the spirit giveth life," was intended to tell us more than the obvious truth that some passages of Scripture had a figurative or typical sense. The "letter" kills us not only by tempting us to miss a meaning. Even when the meaning (whether literal or spiritual) is abundantly clear, even when we fully grasp its implications, it "kills" us if we get no further than *knowledge* of what it means.

The Law tells us: "thou shalt not covet." No hidden sense here. The literal meaning is plain enough. Selfish desires are the root of all evil. But, says St Augustine: to know this truth without conforming our lives to the commandments not to covet, is to be *killed,* by that commandment. If we had never known our responsibility we could not have been held guilty for not living up to it. In order to fulfil the law, we must be dead to the kind of life which the law intends to kill, and live by the new life which the law sets before us. This is a matter not of knowledge but of love. Everyone knows the ten commandments. Few keep them, because few love them. Men do not love the law of God because they cherish a contrary love, a contrary law, in their flesh, which defeats and denies the law of God. Knowing His law, they still fall short of knowing it, because they only possess the wisdom of the flesh, which cannot be subject to the law of God. It is foredoomed to rebel against Him because it has refused, in advance, to love Him.

The law was given by God to manifest the living death of sin, not to cure it. St Augustine's tract *"De Spiritu et Littera"* is therefore not a treatise on the senses of the Scripture but on the law and on Grace. Yet it has most interesting implications for the meaning of Scripture, because charity is the fulfilment of the Law. The Law can only be undertood when it is kept. It cannot be kept unless God drives out the contrary law, the law of selfishness, of cupidity, and infuses into our hearts His selfless charity. Without grace, the "letter" of the Law, the truth of the Law, serves only to condemn us, because even though we understand it we do not keep it. But the "spirit," grace, fills us with charity, gives us the power to love what the Law tells us. Loving the truth, we are able to live by the truth. When we live by the truth our lives themselves become true. We become what we ought to be. We not only exist, we *live*. We not only hear the word, we keep it, and therefore we *fulfil* it. We live in God. God lives in us. His will is done in us. He is manifested in us. He is glorified in us. This was not possible until He sent His Son to be a propitiation for our sins. St. Augustine says:

Where the Holy Spirit does not help us, inspiring us with good desires to replace evil desires, that is to say pouring out Charity in our hearts, it is evident that the Law, good as it may be, by its very prohibition only intensifies our evil desires.[124]

Without the Holy Spirit we can admire the goodness of God and His truth. We can even attempt to see Him. But a love that is not inspired and directed by His Spirit misses its aim, even though it be aimed at Him: for only God can reach God. That is why He sent us His Son, to be the "way." We must then receive His Holy Spirit, the Spirit of Jesus, Who will lead us to God by the power of a secret and spiritual delight in the things of God, by a taste for the hidden truth of God, by love that finds Him in the mystery of a presence that is only secret because it is too blinding in its obviousness to be seen by us. *Accipiat homo Spiritum sanctum quo fiat in animo ejus delectatio dilectioque summi atque incommutabilis boni quod Deus est.*[125]

The outpouring of the Spirit is the fulfilment of the Law the Psalms and the Prophets. When Jesus appeared to His disciples in the cenacle after His resurrection, He told them that it was "necessary for all things to be fulfilled which are written in the Law of Moses and in the Prophets and in the Psalms concerning me."[126]

Then he "opened their understanding" and showed them the "spiritual meaning" of the Scriptures—as well as the letter. What was this fulfilment? Not only the death and Resurrection of Jesus—these were ordered to something else, to His life in us. It was therefore written not only that Christ should "suffer and rise again from the dead the third day" but also that great effects should follow from these things: "that penance and remission of sins should be preached in His name unto all nations beginning at Jerusalem." The charity of the Saints is the fulfilment of the Scriptures. The outpouring of the Holy Spirit makes this a fact, and enables those in whom He acts to understand what has happened. "And you are witnesses of these things. And I send the promise of my Father (the Holy Spirit) upon you: stay you in the city until you be endued with power from on high."[127]

We who chant the Psalms, hope to praise God. We praise Him best if we understand the things we sing. We understand them if we, too, are "endued with power from on high." When the Spirit of Divine Love sets our souls on fire with charity we realize, at last, that it is not necessary for us to scale heaven to bring down Christ to us by some mysterious technique of contemplation. The Liturgy does not have to bring Christ from heaven. It is the manifestation of His presence and His power on earth. It does not have to prepare our hearts for a future Kingdom. It tells us that His Kingdom has already come. *Regnum Dei intra vos est.* It is established in full power in the midst of a godless humanity. Heaven is within us and all around us, even though we seem to be living in hell.

The Psalms are the language of His Kingdom. They were spoken by prophets to those who were able to understand them centuries before the Kingdom was established. They were sung as they were fulfilled by the Saviour as He hung on the Cross, so that the voice of the Psalms is the voice of Christ Himself. He lives in us, being both the Kingdom and its King. And we, when we take His words upon our lips, speak not our thoughts but His, provided that the Spirit of His Promise lives in our own spirit and is the inspiration of our own song.

Therefore, when a Christian chants the Office, if he is fully a

Christian, that is to say if He is one who has attained to the knowledge of Christ, who has experienced what it means to live in the great mystery of Christ, who longs to see all things restored in Christ, then he not only understands the Psalms, but he *fulfils* them. The deep contemplative penetration of the Psalms, is only achieved by their fulfilment. It is the realization of their fulfilment in us. It shows us our own place in the Mystery of Christ, and our own vocation, to make up what is wanting to His sufferings in our own moment of history. But the Psalms are the songs of eternity since His Kingdom is the Kingdom that will never end. In the simultaneous totality of possession, which is what eternity means, the Psalms reach out to possess the reward together with the suffering, the victory in the midst of the battle. We have only begun to fight and yet if we believe in Him Who overcomes the world, we have already won. "For whatsoever is born of God overcomes the world: and this is the victory which overcomes the world, our faith."[128]

Laws, rules and methods are for those who seek to get something for themselves. They therefore savor of this earth and of its slavery, although they are necessary even for those who would begin to be children of the kingdom. But after all, it is not by seeking to "get something out of the Psalms" that we will finally arrive at an understanding of the Psalter or of our Canonical Office. Although the Psalms are given us for our benefit it is not enough to think only of our own benefit: they are first of all for the glory of God. God is glorified most in those who have given up everything for Him and have found everything in Him. The Psalms profit us most when they give God most Glory. This they do when we realize that the Liturgy is not a search for something we have not, but the celebration of what we already have.

The Psalms are the new song, the *canticum novum,* the song of those who have been reborn in a new creation, the song of those for whom there is no law, because in them Christ has fulfilled the Law. How, then, should the Psalms offer them a method, a technique, that is to say a "law" of contemplation? The true meaning of the Psalms is most fully apprehended by those who have been swept, by an experience of God's mercy, beyond the reach of any rule or any method. The new song of the Psalms is the song of God's children who live by no other rule than God their Father, Who is His own Rule. He is also therefore theirs. His love is their Law. They always do what is pleasing Him. Thus for them there is no law, not because the law has been abrogated but because it has been perfectly fulfilled.

Author's Note:

In dealing with the spiritual sense of Scripture in this book, it has been my intention to follow as closely as possible the norms laid down in recent Papal documents, especially the Encyclical *Divino Afflante Spiritu*. If my ignorance and stupidity have led me to misinterpret the teaching of the Church, I wish it to be known that I renounce any error that I may have made. In places where I have presumed to hold that any particular Scriptural text had a spiritual sense, and where I have expressed some opinion regarding that sense, I invite those who strongly disagree with my interpretation to disregard my opinion and to act as if I were merely making a pious application of the text. They will then, I hope, be more inclined to see and appreciate the practical consequences of my opinions in the life of prayer.

Notes:

1 *Acts of the Apostles*, 17 : 24–28.

2 *John*, 17 : 3.

3 *The Way of Perfection*, Chapter 30.

4 *Ibid.*, Chapter 37.

5 *Ibid.* See especially Chapters 25, 26, 27.

6 Cassian, *Collatio*, I, iv. *Patrologia Latina*, Volume 49, Column 486.

7 *Patrologia Latina*, Volume 6, Column 489.

8 *Collatio* xiv, 10; Translation from Owen Chadwick, *John Cassian.* Cambridge, 1950.

9 *Ibid.* xiv, 10. cf. *Leviticus*, 26 : 12 and *II Corinthians*, 6 : 16.

10 *De Coenobiorum Institutis*, II, 11. *Patrologia Latina*, Volume 49, Column 100.

11 *Collatio*, IX, 31. *Patrologia Latina*, Volume 49, Column 808. "*Non est perfecta oratio in qua se monachus vel hoc ipsum quod orat intelligit.*"

12 *Collatio*, IX, 25. *Patrologia Latina*, Volume 49, Column 801.

13 " The soul that is athirst for God."—St Bernard.

14 *Psalm* 105.

15 *Psalm* 1, 1–3.

16 *Psalm* 143, 12–15.

17 *John*, 3 : 14.

18 *Acts of the Apostles*, 2 : 29–31.

19 *Divino Afflante Spiritu*, nn. 26–27. N.C.W.C. edition of English translation emanating from the Vatican.

20 See Jean Daniélou *Bible et Liturgie*, Paris, 1951, and *Sacramentum Futuri*, Paris, 1950.

21 *The Ascent to Truth*, New York, 1951, p. 302, cf. also an important article " Scripture in the Spiritual Theology of St John of the Cross," by Fr. Barnabas Mary Ahearn in *Catholic Biblical Quarterly*, Volume 14, n.1, p. 6.

22 *I Corinthians* 2 : 11–12.

23 *Mediator Dei* (November 4, 1947).

24 *Ibid.*, Part III.

25 *The Living Flame of Love*, III, 38; translated by Peers, Volume III, 181.

26 " Expleto Opere Dei omnes cum summo silentio excant, et agatur reverentia Deo, ut Frater, qui forte sibi peculiariter vult orare, non impediatur alterius improbitate."—*Rule of St Benedict*, Chapter 52. Cf. Chapter 20 : " Brevis debet esse et pura oratio : nisi forte ex affectu inspirationis divinae gratiæ protendatur."

27 Cf. *The Roman Missal* : Collect for the Mass of the Dedication of a Church.

28 *Psalm* 18, 2–7.

29 *Psalm* 148, 1–13.

30 Cf. *Romans*, 1 : 18 and *Acts*, 14 : 15.

31 I am especially indebted to the article of Père Jean Daniélou, S. J.: " The Problem of Symbolism " in *Thought*, September, 1950. See also his book *Sacramentum Futuri*, Paris, 1950.

32 The classical passage in this connection is the first chapter of St Paul's *Epistle to the Romans*.

33 *Romans*, 1 : 18.

34 *Romans*, 1 : 25.

35 *Psalm* 8, 2, 4–10. Every line of this Psalm has anti-polytheistic repercussions. Man, who can see God *through* His creation is in possession of the truth which makes him free. (*John*, 8 : 32). Thus he leads a spiritualized existence " a little less than the angels " and stands in his rightful place in the order of creation, above the irrational animals. The Gentiles, on the other hand, have descended lower than the animals since they have lost the knowledge of God though God remains evident in His creation. For by their ignorance of God, they have doomed themselves to the worship of beasts. (*Romans*, 1 : 23). Compare also: St Bernard; *De Diligendo Deo*. Chapter II, n. 4; *Patrologia Latina*, Volume 182, Column 970.

36 *Isaias*, 53 : 6.

37 *Hebrews*, 4 : 12.

38 *John*, 5 : 39–40.

39 *Romans*, 10 : 4, 8–9.

40 *John*, 1 : 45.

41 *Enarratio in Psalmum*, 93, Paragraph 1. *Patrologia Latina*, Volume 37, Column 1189.

42 *Psalm* 68, 1–4.

43 *Psalm* 68, 14–15.

44 *Psalm* 31, 36–67.

45 *John*, 3 : 27.

46 *John*, 1 : 33.

47 *John*, 1 : 12.

48 *Ephesians*, 2 : 5–6.

49 " Grant, we beseech Thee, almighty God, that we who believe Thine only begotten Son to have ascended this day into heaven, may also ourselves dwell in spirit in heavenly places."—*The Roman Missal*: Collect for Ascension Day.

50 ". . . ut quae visibilis mysteriis sumenda percepimus, invisibili consequamur effectu."—*The Roman Missal*: Postcommunion for Ascension Day.

51 " God who of old in many ways spoke to the Father in the Prophets
has lastly in these days spoken to us in His Son . . ."—*Hebrews*, 1 : 1.

52 " Do you not know that as many of us as have been baptized in Christ
Jesus, are baptized in his death? We are buried together with Him by
Baptism in death in order that, just as Christ rose from the dead by the
glory of the Father, we also might walk in newness of life. For if we
are sown in the likeness of His death, we shall share in the likeness of
His Resurrection. . . But if we are dead with Christ, we believe
that we shall also live with Christ, knowing that Christ, rising from the
dead, dieth now no more, and death shall no longer have dominion
over Him, because He died to sin, He died once; but because He lives,
He lives unto God. So you also, consider yourselves as dead to sin but
living unto God in Christ Jesus our Lord."—*Romans*, 6 : 3—11.

53 *Matthew*, 10 : 38–39.

54 *John*, 17 : 23.

55 The term *res sacramenti* is a technical one, used to distinguish the mere
external conferring of a Sacrament (*sacramentum tantum*) from the notion
of the Sacrament considered as fully and concretely realizing the
purpose of its institution by a fruitful production of its signified effect.

56 St Leo : *Sermon lxiii. Patrologia Latina*, Volume 84, Column 357. He is
speaking of Baptism, but the same is true *a fortiori* of the Holy Eucharist.

57 *Ibid.*

58 *Ibid.*

59 See *Hebrews*, 3. Compare also : *I Corinthians*, 10 : 6, 11.

60 *I Corinthians*, 10 : 4.

61 *Numbers*, 24 : 2–9.

62 *I Peter*, 2 : 21.

63 " Jerusalem quae aedificatur ut civitas, cujus participatio ejus in
idipsum : illi enim ascenderunt tribus, tribus Domini, testimonium
Israel ad confitendum nomini Domini."—*Psalm* 121 : 3–4.

64 *Galatians*, 6 : 14.

65 " The charity of God is poured forth in our hearts by the Holy Spirit
Who is given to us."—*Romans*, 5 : 5.

66 *I Corinthians*, 2 : 6–10.

67 St John of the Cross : *The Living Flame of Love*, Stanza I, n. 15.

68 *Enarratio in Psalmum*, 30, Paragraph 4.

69 *In Epistolam, Joannis ad Parthos*, Tractatus V, Chapter 5, Paragraph 3.
Patrologia Latina, Volume 35, Column 2055.

70 *Enarratio in Psalmum*, 61. *Patrologia Latina*, Volume 36, Column 730.
It is the teaching of the Fathers that we are all originally created
mystically as " one man " and that this " Person", divided by the

sin of Adam, is reconstituted in one mystical Body in Christ, the new Adam. Compare St Cyril of Alexandria, in *Evangelium Joannis*, *i*, " Sumus omnes in Christo, et communis humanitatis persona in ipsum revivisciti."

71 " A finibus terrae ad te clamavi."—*Psalm*, 60 : 3.

72 The " Gradual Psalms " are the group from Psalm 119 to 133 inclusive. Each one is entitled " Canticum graduum " in the Vulgate.

73 *Matthew*, 5 : 5.

74 *De Civitate Dei*, XIV, 25.

75 *De Civitate Dei*, XIV, 26. The terms " blessedness " and " fruition " are of course only relative here.

76 *Psalm* 39 : 7–9.

77 *Galatians*, 5 : 13 and 17.

78 *Galatians*, 5 : 13 and 17.

79 *Romans*, 10 : 4.

80 *Romans*, 13 : 10.

81 *James*, 1 : 25.

82 " Causa diligendi, Deum Deus est, modus sine modo diligere,"— St Bernard : *De Diligendo Deo*, I : 1.

83 " Lex Domini immaculata convertens animas "—*Psalm* 18 : 8. It is not for us to enter into a technical discussion of the fact that perhaps for the author of the Psalms the word " law " may have meant the Law of Moses. Since the establishment of the New Testament the Fathers of the Church have taken it in St Paul's higher sense : with the consequence that St Ambrose's commentary on Psalm 118 (the longest Psalm, and all in praise of the " Law ") becomes a treatise on the mystical Love of God in which Psalm 118 is considered as if it were the equivalent of the Canticle of Canticles.

84 " Delectabit sane non tam nostra vel sopita necessitas vel sortita felicitas, quam quod ejus in nobis et de nobis voluntas adimpleta videbitur, quod et quotidie postulamus in oratione cum dicimus fiat voluntas tua sicut in coelo et in terra."—St Bernard : *De Diligendo Deo*, X, 28.

85 See *Matthew*, 5 : 17–20.

86 *Matthew*, 5 : 20.

87 *Psalm*, 35 : 7. St John of the Cross gives much the same interpretation of " judicia Domini vera " (*Psalm* 18 : 10—11). *The Ascent to the Cross* II, 26.

88 *Psalm*, 23 : 3–6.

89 See St Augustine : *De Sermone Domini in Monte*. St Thomas Aquinas, II, IIae, Q. 8, a.7.

90   *De Diligendo Deo*, XII, 34.

91   *II Paralipomenon*, 5 : 13.

92   *II Paralipomenon*, 20 : 20–21.

93   *II Paralipomenon*, 20 : 24.

94   *Galatians*, 5: 23.

95   *I Kings*, 23 : 14.

96   *Psalm* 53 : 6–8.

97   *Enarratio in Psalmum* 53, Paragraph 10.

98   *Psalm* 136 : 4.

99   *Loc cit.* Note that it is no sin *not* to love God gratuitously. But this " freedom " is the perfection of love.

100   *Luke*, 24 : 16, 32, 31.

101   I only wish here to make a legitimate application of this Gospel text. Although the first example taken is probably a literal expression of the experience of " living faith ", the second is not precisely what I mean by mystical contemplation since it was, probably, a grace of the order of " gratiae gratis datae " and, in any case, it was a vision. The mystical contemplation which concerns us here is an experience of God in obscurity, a recognition that is not achieved by the senses or through the medium of any species, intelligible or otherwise. The second Gospel example, then, is used here only as an analogy.

102   *Luke*, 24 : 31.

103   This is another of the key texts in the Mystical Theology of Christ's discourse at the Last Supper. "In that day you shall know that I am in my Father and you in me and I in you."—*John*, 14 : 20. We are not here speaking of a formal illumination of the intellect such as is enjoyed by the blessed in Heaven. This is not an immediate intuition of God as He is in Himself, face to face, but an immediate experience of God by contact of love, in darkness.

104   *Philippians*, 2 : 5–10.

105   *Psalm* 21 : 13–16.

106   *Psalm* 87, 1–4, 7–9.

107   *Colossians*, 3 : 3.

108   *The Roman Missal*. Blessing of The Paschal Candle, Holy Saturday.

109   *Psalm* 16 : 8.

110   *Psalm* 16 : 8. Compare also : *The Cistercian Breviary:* Versicle for Compline.

111   *Psalm* 90 : 15.

112   *Psalm* 120 : 1.

113   *Acts*, 14 : 21.

114   *John*, 12 : 24.

115 *John*, 11 : 50–52. Gospel for Friday in Passion Week.
116 *Psalm* 30 : 21 " Abscondisti eos in abscondito facie tuae."
117 *Psalm* 30 : 21.
118 *Genesis*, 11 : 7.
119 St Augustine : *De Civitate Dei*, XIV, 28.
120 *Luke*, 22 : 15.
121 *Matthew*, 26 : 29.
122 *I Corinthians*, 14 : 15
123 I IIae. Q.106. A.1. and St Augustine, *De Spiritu et Littera*, 26.
124 *De Spiritu et Littera*, Chapter iv.
125 *Ibid.*, Chapter iii.
126 *Luke*, 24 : 44.
127 *Luke*, 24 : 48–49.
128 *I John*, 5 : 4.